Study Guide

Noel Barker
DePaul University

Racial and Ethnic Groups

Eighth Edition

Richard T. Schaefer

DePaul University

PRENTICE HALL, Upper Saddle River, New Jersey 07458

©2000 by PRENTICE-HALL, INC.
Upper Saddle River, New Jersey 07458

ISBN-0 321-05028-2

Printed in the United States of America

Contents

CHAPTER 1

Understanding Race and Ethnicity

I. LEARNING OBJECTIVES

1. To become familiar with the factors that determine what is a dominant and what is a subordinate group.
2. To understand the role of power and privilege in relations between a minority and a majority.
3. To learn about the four types of subordinate groups.
4. To become familiar with the complexity and the social importance of race.
5. To be introduced to the different sociological perspectives regarding intergroup relations.
6. To understand the importance of the processes that create dominant/subordinate groups.

II. CHAPTER OVERVIEW

In this chapter Schaefer discusses the role of power and privilege in majority relations with a minority, introducing you to the characteristics that define a minority group as well as the social construction and social significance of race categories. Furthermore, you are introduced to the theoretical perspectives of the functionalists, conflict theorists and labeling theorists. This chapter also discusses the creation of dominant and subordinate groups.

A. What Is a Subordinate Group? This section discusses the role of power in defining a minority or subordinate group. In addition, the five characteristics of subordinate groups are outlined.
1. What is the sociological role of power in the definition of a minority or subordinate group?
2. How does societal power determine one's life opportunities?
3. What are the five characteristics of a subordinate group? Why are these characteristics significant to our understanding of relations between dominant and subordinate groups?
4. Are there groups that you consider to be minority or subordinate groups that don't meet all five characteristics? Explain how you see these groups to be minorities or subordinate.

B. Types of Subordinate Groups. This section introduces the four types of minority or subordinate groups and how these types fit the five characteristics of minority or subordinate groups mentioned in the previous section.
1. What are the four types of minority or subordinate groups?
2. Explain how racial groups differ from ethnic groups.
3. Explain why sociologists consider Jewish people to belong to an ethnic group rather than a religious group.

C. Race. In this section you will be introduced to the idea that race is a socially constructed concept.
1. In order to have biologically significant races, what would they have to be?
2. If there were significant differences between the races, what would this mean?
3. Why is race significant?

4. What is racial formation? Give an example of this process that is not offered in your text.

D. Sociology and the Study of Race and Ethnicity. This section introduces you to the concept of stratification as well as the different sociological perspectives of dominant relations to subordinates.
1. What is stratification and how does it relate to Weber's concept of class?
2. How can annexation affect the culture of the minority group?
3. What is colonialism? What is the relationship between colonizers and the colony?
4. How does the labeling theory relate to the conflict perspective?
5. How can the concept of the self-fulfilling prophecy be used to explain the lower standard of living of members of subordinate groups?

E. The Creation of Subordinate Group Status. In this section you are introduced to the situations that lead to the formation of subordinate groups. The way in which a subordinate group forms greatly influences and is greatly influenced by the perceptions of that group as well as the power that group possesses.
1. What are the two types of factors that influence migration? Give an example of each not mentioned in your text.
2. How can annexation affect the culture of the minority group?
3. What is colonialism? What is the relationship between colonizers and the colony?

F. The Consequences of Subordinate-Group Status. This section outlines the six consequences of subordinate group status.
1. Define extermination. What other terms for extermination have been created?
2. What leads to expulsion? Give an example not mentioned in your text.
3. What is secession? How does it affect the status of a subordinate group?
4. What is segregation? How is segregation imposed on subordinate groups by the dominant group in the U. S.?
5. How does fusion relate to amalgamation?
6. What role must the member of a subordinate group take in the process of assimilation? What factors influence the speed with which assimilation takes place?

G. Pluralist Perspective. Not all dominant relations with subordinates lead to the removal of the subordinate group. This section introduces you to pluralism and the factors necessary for such a relation to exist.
1. What is pluralism? What does it imply?
2. What does a relationship of pluralism allow minority groups to do?
3. What does a pluralist believe?
4. What is bilingualism? How do pluralists view it? What perspective would someone opposed to bilingualism hold?

H. Who Am I? This section discusses the continual process of racial formation, the importance of naming and the emergence of panethnicity.
1. What are some of the implications of changing names for racial and ethnic groups?
2. What is panethnicity? Give an example that is not provided in the your text.
3. According to your text, what are some of the implications of panethnic labels?

4. What is marginality? What are the factors that lead to such a status?

I. Resistance and Change. This section introduces resistance by subordinate groups to the actions of the majority. These issues will be addressed in greater detail later in the text.
1. How does resistance by subordinate groups manifest itself?
2. What is the Afrocentric perspective? What does it work toward? How is it viewed by opponents and supporters?

III. CRITICAL THINKING QUESTIONS

1. Would assimilation or pluralism be more beneficial for U.S. society? How would each situation be viewed by a functionalist and a conflict theorist? Explain your answer, supporting your assertions which material from the text wherever appropriate.
2. What is your race? What is your ethnicity? Which do you feel to be the most important? Why? Do you ever feel that you are treated differently because of you race or ethnicity? Is this treatment favorable or unfavorable? How does this influence or how is this influenced by your power in society? Please explain your answer.
3. What might prevent a group that is in the majority from being dominant in a society?

IV. KEY TERMS

Listed below are some of the key terms introduced in Chapter 1. After having read the chapter and completed the overview on the previous pages, check your comprehension of these terms by writing down the definitions in the space provided in your own words. You can review your work by directing your attention to the Key Terms section at the end of your text.

Afrocentric perspective
amalgamation
assimilation
bilingualism
biological race
class
colonialism
conflict perspective
dysfunction
emigration
ethnic cleansing
ethnic group
functionalist perspective
fusion
genocide
immigration
intelligence quotient
internal colonialism
labeling theory

marginality
melting pot
migration
minority group
panethnicity
pluralism
racial formation
racial group
racism
segregation
self-fulfilling prophecy
sociology
stereotypes
stratification
world systems theory

V. TEST QUESTIONS

Multiple Choice Questions
Choose the correct answer from the choices provided.

1. Which of the following is NOT a characteristic of a subordinate group?
a. awareness of subordination
b. unequal treatment
c. different values from the dominant group
d. involuntary membership

2. William G. Sumner noted that individuals make distinctions between members of their own group and those of:
a. the majority
b. the other
c. the status quo
d. the out group

3. Which of the following is considered an ethnic group?
a. Catholics
b. Jews
c. Texans
d. Muslims

4. The term racial group refers to:
a. those who are classified according to obvious physical differences.
b. those who are classified according to genetic differences.
c. those who are classified according to national origin.
d. those who are classified according to obvious cultural differences.

5. Which sociologist indicated that "the problem of the twentieth century is the problem of the colorline?"
a. C. W. Mills
b. Max Weber
c. W. E. B. Du Bois
d. William Julius Wilson

6. Biologically, races are:
a. pure and distinct.
b. predictors of intelligence.
c. not mutually exclusive.
d. determined by blood type.

7. According to sociologists, a society that is characterized by members having unequal amounts of wealth, prestige, or power is said to be:
a. classified.
b. stratified.
c. dysfunctional.
d. unfair.

8. According to functionalists, which of the following is NOT one of the four functions that racial beliefs have for the dominant group?
a. Racist ideologies provide a moral justification for maintaining a stratified society.
b. Racist beliefs provide a cause for political action.
c. Racist myths encourage support for the existing social order.
d. Racist beliefs encourage subordinate people to question their status.

9. In their book *The Bell Curve*, Herrnstein and Murray claim that:
a. all intelligence is inherited.
b. all racial groups are equally intelligent.
c. race and IQ are linked attributes.
d. intelligence is environmental.

10. The distinctive pattern of oppression between members of the dominant and subordinate groups within the same country is called:
a. internal colonialism.
b. secession.
c. segregation.
d. racism.

True/False Questions
For each of the following statements, determine whether it is true or false. Write your answer in the space provided.

1. Hispanics can be Black or White.

2. According to researchers, most genetic variations occur within racial categories rather than between racial categories.

3. Racial formation is determined by those who have societal power within a racially stratified system.

4. According to the functionalist perspective, racist beliefs threaten the stability of society.

5. Segregation no longer exists in the U.S.

6. Annexation leads to the suppression of the language and culture of the minority.

7. Secession leads to a subordinate group becoming a dominant group.

8. Pluralists and integrationists seek the elimination of ethnic boundaries.

9. Racial and ethnic categories are socially constructed and are thus flexible and subject to change.

10. By bringing Black and White activists together, the civil rights movement fostered panethnicity in the United States.

Completion
Write in the word or words that best completes each of the following statements:

1. Sociologists define a _____ _____ as a group whose members have significantly less control or power over their own lives.

2. _____ _____ are groups set apart from others because of their national origin or distinctive cultural patterns.

3. _____ _____ theory views the global economic system as divided between nations that control wealth and those that provide natural resources and labor.

4. The hierarchy that emerges in societies that are characterized by members having unequal amounts of wealth, prestige or power is called _____.

5. According to the _____ _____, the parts of society are structured to maintain its stability and serve both as functions and _____.

6. Howard Becker introduced the concept of the _____ _____ to try to explain why certain people are viewed as different from or less worthy than others.

7. When we respond to negative stereotypes and act on them with the result that false definitions become accurate, this is known as a _____ _____.

8. _____ describes leaving a country to settle in another, _____ denotes coming into the new country.

9. The result when a minority group and a majority group combine to form a new group is known as _____.

10. The status of being between two cultures is known as _____. Incomplete assimilation also results in this.

Essay Questions.
Answer the following questions to the best of your ability. Be sure to support your answers thoroughly.

1. Describe in detail both the functionalist and the conflict perspective on racial stratification. In your opinion, which perspective most accurately explains racist beliefs? Explain your answer and support your assertions.

2. In what different ways do subordinate groups come to be treated? How does the way in which a subordinate group is formed affect its relationship to the dominant group? How does it shape the opportunities of the members of the subordinate group? Give examples and explain your answer.

3. Why does incomplete assimilation most often lead to marginality? What sociological theory best explains this? Provide examples not offered in your text to illustrate your answer.

Prejudice

I. LEARNING OBJECTIVES

1. To understand how prejudice plays a role in perceptions of people seen as racially "different."
2. To become familiar with the similarities and differences between prejudice and discrimination.
3. To explore various theories and explanations of prejudice, including exploitation theory, scapegoat theory, authoritarian personality theory, and normative theory.
4. To identify some possibilities that lead to a reduction of prejudice between groups.

II. CHAPTER OBJECTIVES

Chapter Two focuses on the causes and effects of prejudice between various races and ethnic groups. Schaefer introduces theories of prejudice, methods of studying its impact on individuals and groups, and the common stereotypes and perceptions that prejudice encourages. This serves as an overview of how sociologists explain this phenomenon, and how it is exacerbated or reduced.

A. Hate Crimes. This section introduces the concept of crimes motivated by bias.
1. How does the federal government define hate crimes?
2. What has the federal government done so far against hate crimes?

B. Prejudice and Discrimination. This section explores the differences between prejudice and discrimination. Various theories and studies are presented to illustrate how these concepts are different.
1. What is the difference between prejudice and discrimination? How are they similar?
2. Explain the four categories of prejudice and discrimination according to Merton. How does his formulation help us to understand these two concepts?
3. What were the findings in the LaPiere study? How might Merton explain why this occurred?

C. Theories of Prejudice. This section introduces four different theories of why prejudice exists as a social phenomenon. Each theory has its strengths and weaknesses.
1. Briefly define each of the following four theories of prejudice:
Exploitation Theory
Scapegoat Theory
Authoritarian Personality Theory
Normative Approach

2. List the strengths and weaknesses of each theory:

	Strengths	Weaknesses
Exploitation		
Scapegoat		
Authoritarian Personality		
Normative		

3. Explain the caste approach. To which of the above theories is it related and why?

D. The Content of Prejudice: Stereotypes. Stereotypes play an important role in our understanding of prejudice, as they shape our views of different groups. This section show us that while common perceptions have changed over time, it is difficult to measure the stereotypes people hold.
1. What are stereotypes, and how do they arise?
2. What does recent research on stereotypes in the U.S. reveal? Has stereotyping changed over the years?
3. Discuss the relationship between stereotyping and self-fulfilling prophecy.

E. The Extent of Prejudice. Like stereotypes, the extent of prejudice in society is challenging to study empirically. The social distance scale is a useful tool for measuring prejudice and attitude change over time.
1. What are some of the reasons that prejudice is difficult to measure?
2. How does the social distance scale attempt to measure prejudice? What are the tentative conclusions we can draw based on the study's results over time?
3.. What are some of the causes of attitude change?

F. Mood of the Subordinate Group. Although traditionally social scientists have argued that having a minority status causes low self-esteem in individuals, in this section we learn why this view is now challenged.
1. What is Du Bois' opinion of the experience of subordinate groups as shown by his metaphor of the "veil"?
2. How do different racial groups perceive race relations differently?
3. What is the rationale behind the argument that subordinates suffer from self-hate and low self-esteem? What is Bloom's disagreement with this belief?

G. Intergroup Hostility. While we often think of Whites as holding negative stereotypes of minority groups, we learn here that subordinate groups hold such perceptions of each other as well. In addition, these stereotypes of others are not always negative.
1. List some examples of positive and negative views of certain racial groups held by others.
2. What are some possible functions of these attitudes?

H. Arab Americans and American Muslims: A Case Study of Emerging Prejudice. As our nation's diversity continues to grow, so do the prejudices we hold. In this section, we see how two small yet expanding groups illustrate how prejudice emerges in our culture.

1. According to the author, what are some reasons why prejudice against Arab Americans and American Muslims has been increasing?
2. List three recent events that illustrate prejudice against these two groups.

I. Reducing Prejudice. Most people would agree that prejudice is wrong and should be eliminated. This section presents mass media, education, and contact theory as possibilities for reducing prejudice.
3. What are the challenges to and possibilities for reducing prejudice?
4. What are some examples that show the mass media as an effective tool in reducing prejudice? What are some examples that who how it can cause prejudice to increase?
5. Discuss how education, both formal and informal, can affect attitudes on race.
6. What is the contact hypothesis? What are some barriers to its manifestation?

III. CRITICAL THINKING QUESTIONS

1. This chapter opens by listing recent events that illustrate prejudice and discrimination in the U.S. Discuss two similar examples from your hometown or campus community. Which of the four theories of prejudice do you think best explains why these incidents occurred? Be sure to show why you think the other three fall short.

2. We often point our fingers at the mass media for perpetuating prejudice. What does this author cite as the possible influences of the mass media and why? Do you think the media are potentially more helpful or harmful in reducing prejudice? Use current examples to defend your position.

IV. KEY TERMS

Listed below are some of the key terms introduced in Chapter 2. After having read the chapter and completed the overview on the previous pages, check your comprehension of these terms by writing down the definitions in the space provided in your own words. You can review your work by directing your attention to the Key Terms section at the end of your text.

authoritarian personality
Bogardus scale
caste approach
contact hypothesis
discrimination
ethnocentrism
ethnophaulism
exploitation theory
normative approach
prejudice
scapegoat

V. TEST QUESTIONS

Multiple Choice Questions
Choose the correct answer from the choices provided.

1. Ethnocentrism is:
a. the belief that having an ethnicity is essential to one's identity.
b. the tendency to assume that one's culture and way of life are superior to all others.
c.. the fear of those unlike oneself.
d. the belief that every city should have an ethnic center.

2. The main difference between prejudice and discrimination is that:
a. prejudice refers to actions, and discrimination to belief.
b. we may be prejudiced towards those like us, but discriminate against those who are different.
c. prejudice refers to beliefs, while discrimination refers to actions.
d. they are really one and the same; there is no difference.

3. Exploitation theory is related to which school of sociological thought?
a. Marxism
b. functionalism
c. normative sociology
d. none of the above

4. The authoritarian personality theory of prejudice focuses on what as the cause of prejudice feeling?
a. the influence of those in positions of authority
b. personality traits of individuals
c. the way the personalities of those in different ethnic groups interact with each other to create prejudice
d. prejudice as a normal social phenomenon

5. Author Brent Staples found that he easily created fear amongst others, especially white women, when walking at night. His response was to:
a. avoid walking at night.
b. wear a tie and carry a briefcase.
c. whistle classical music.
d. scare people deliberately.

6. Two common stereotypes of Arabs as shown in a 1993 survey are that:
a. they are all in the oil industry and have darker complexions.
b. they are all Muslim and support terrorism against non-believers.
c. they support terrorism and suppress women.
d. they all ride camels and live in tents.

7. In response to violent crimes motivated by prejudice, the federal government has:
a. outlawed hate groups.
b. raised the minimum penalties for these crimes.
c. emphasized the importance of free speech.
d. gathered statistics on the problem.

8. The fact that a third of high school students surveyed in 1988 thought that depictions of African American life on TV were real and accurate shows us:
a. the strong influence of television on people's perceptions.
b. other forms of media are actually more influential in shaping stereotypes.
c. that racial depictions in the media have changed little over time.
d. TV really does do a good job in portraying racial minorities.

9. The contact hypothesis states that:
a. intergroup contact perpetuates racism.
b. when people of different groups interact harmoniously and in equal status, prejudice will be reduced.
c. when different people come into contact, they use stereotypes to judge each other.
d. people only like to interact with those like themselves.

10. While this chapter presents four main theories of prejudice, the author maintains that which offers the best explanation?
a. Exploitation theory
b. Normative theory
c. A combination of scapegoat and authoritarian personality theories.
d. None of the above, he states that no one theory is sufficient.

True/False Questions
For each of the following statements, determine whether it is true or false. Write your answer in the space provided.

1. Prejudice and discrimination are one and the same.

2. The Chinese couple in LaPiere's study were not discriminated against at public establishments even though the staff of these places stated they would deny service to Chinese people.

3. The caste approach describes a system where social inequality is inherited.

4. The normative theory of prejudice states that people use others unfairly for economic advantage.

5. Stereotypes are held by both dominant and subordinate groups.

6. All sociologists agree that members of subordinate groups tend to suffer from self-hate and low self-esteem.

7. All Muslims are of Arabic decent.

8. Formal education is associated with racial tolerance.

9. Studies show that bringing people together with a common goal does little to reduce intergroup hostility.

10. One barrier to equal-status contact is that our society is highly segregated.

Completion
Write in the word or words that best completes the following statements:

1. _____ is another word for ethnic slurs.

2. Merton's formulation shows _____ different interactions between prejudice and discrimination.

3. The _____ theory of prejudice states that people are prejudiced because they feel like victims and want to blame another group for their problems.

4. The Bogardus scale, also known as the _____ _____ scale attempts to measure the extent of prejudice.

5. _____ exists not only between dominant and subordinate groups, but also among specific subordinate groups.

6. Arabs are a (n) _____ group while Muslims are a (n) _____ group.

7.Muslim women wearing headscarves, or _____, have encountered harassment and discrimination.

8. Federal law prohibits hate crimes only if they violate a federally guaranteed right such as

_____.

9. _____ _____ and _____ influence levels of prejudice as they are major elements of our social environment.

10. Two key factors in reducing hostility between groups are _____
_____ _____ and the presence of a _____
_____.

Essay Questions

Answer the following questions to the best of your ability. Be sure to support your answers thoroughly.

1. This chapter focuses on mass media, education, and equal-status contact as influences in reducing prejudice between groups. Briefly explain how each of these three phenomena have the potential to minimize prejudice. Which of these could be the most influential, in your opinion? Be sure to explain and defend your position carefully. Which theory of prejudice (exploitative, normative, scapegoat, or authoritarian personality) would see the solution to prejudice in the influence you have chosen? Why?

2. Sociologists disagree about how minority status affects the "mood of the subordinate group." Briefly summarize the opposing viewpoints as stated in the text. Which position do you find most plausible? Explain why this makes the most sense to you and the others don't, relying on information from the book as well as examples from your own experience. Does looking to the mood of the dominant group help us to understand these theories differently?

3. In Chapter 2, Arab Americans and American Muslims are given as examples of two groups targeted by emerging prejudice. Are there other groups that have also been recently attached? What makes you think so? What methods of reducing prejudice would be most likely to help? What prevents this from happening?

CHAPTER 3

Discrimination

I. LEARNING OBJECTIVES

1. To understand some of the explanations of why discrimination occurs.
2. To become familiar with the institutional factors that perpetuate inequality.
3. To learn about the factors which can exacerbate one's subordinate status.
4. To understand the origins and purposes of affirmative action programs.
5. To become familiar with the ways in which members of subordinate groups respond to situations of institutional discrimination.

II. CHAPTER OVERVIEW

Building from what you learned in the previous chapter, this chapter focuses on the institutional factors that perpetuate inequalities experienced by members of subordinate groups. It also looks at programs instituted to attempt to correct these discriminatory policies, and the debates currently surrounding such programs. Finally, this chapter outlines the institutional conditions limiting the successes of minority individuals, as well as how members of subordinate groups work to overcome these barriers.

A. Understanding Discrimination. This section introduces the concept of discrimination, distinguishing between relative and absolute deprivation, and discussing the important concepts of total and institutional discrimination.
1. What is it that conflict theorists say determines deprivation and oppression? In your own words, explain why they argue this.
2. What is the difference between relative and absolute deprivation? How does this help you to understand the level of discrimination currently faced by minorities in the United States?
3. What does the term total discrimination refer to? According to the text, why is it not enough, when considering discrimination, to focus only on what is being done to people now?
4. What is the difference between individual discrimination and institutional discrimination? Why would the latter be considered to be more significant?
5. Using the concept of institutional racism, explain how discrimination can take place without an individual's intention to deprive others from privileges.
6. What institutional policies or practices at your university or place of work could be considered examples of institutional discrimination? Explain your answer.

B. Informal Economy. This section focuses on the role of past discrimination in perpetuating an informal economy and a dual labor market.
1. What does the term informal economy refer to? How is it significant to the issue of discrimination?

2. According to conflict theorists, how does a dual labor market affect the competition between dominant and subordinate groups? In your own words, discuss how this influences one's life opportunities. Explain your answer.

3. Explain how past discrimination leads to a self-fulfilling cycle that perpetuates an informal economy.

C. The Underclass. In this section you are introduced to the concept of the underclass and the structural factors that contribute to the increase of those living at this social stratum.

1. What is the underclass? What are the structural factors that contribute to its growth?

2. According to the text, what are two positions regarding the cause of the underclass? Which do you think provides the best explanation? Support your answer.

D. Discrimination Today. This section offers examples of the presence of institutional discrimination and the informal economy. In addition, it addresses the difficulties in quantifying discrimination as well as agents of social change that can work toward reducing discrimination.

1. What is double jeopardy? According to the text, have the ramifications of double jeopardy gotten better or gotten worse over the last 50 years?

2. What are some of the factors of past discrimination that influence the present social position of African Americans or Hispanics?

3. What factors besides education are responsible for the income gap between Whites and Blacks? Explain why these factors are significant.

E. Environmental Justice. This section introduces the concept of environmental justice, and explains how environmental factors can affect intergroup relations.

1. Why are low-income and minority neighborhoods more likely to be adjacent to waste sites?

2. What are some of the arguments against the concept of environmental racism?

F. Affirmative Action. This section explains affirmative action as a tool for reducing institutional discrimination. In addition, the key debates surrounding affirmative action policies are discussed.

1. What is affirmative action? According to the text, how are affirmative action efforts effective in dealing with current and past discrimination?

2. What is reverse discrimination? Considering the information provided in the text, do you think affirmative action policies have resulted in reverse discrimination? Again, using information provided in the text, support your answer.

3. In your opinion, what is the best mechanism for reducing institutional discrimination: affirmative action programs or color-blind policies? Support your answer using information provided in the text.

G. The Glass Ceiling. This section introduces the concepts of glass ceilings and glass walls, discussing their relation to the occupational mobility and economic success of women and minority men.

1. What is the glass ceiling? What are a few of the glass ceiling barriers?

2. What are glass walls? How are the barriers associated with glass walls related to gender stereotypes?

3. Urban League President John Jacob said that Blacks can do only so much for themselves; self-development cannot succeed without an "opportunity environment." What does he mean by this? Incorporate concepts such as past discrimination, glass ceilings and walls, as well as the notion of affirmative action in your answer.

III. CRITICAL THINKING QUESTIONS

1. Considering debates surrounding affirmative action programs, what do you see as the most effective solution to reducing if not eliminating institutional discrimination? Explain your answer, supporting your assertions with material from the text wherever appropriate.

2. At your own college or university how well do the faculty and student bodies reflect the racial and sex composition of the area and the nation? Do you see evidence of institutional discrimination? Explain your answer.

IV. KEY TERMS

Listed below are some of the key terms introduced in Chapter 3. After having read the chapter and completed the overview on the previous pages, check your comprehension of these terms by writing down the definitions in the space provided in your own words. You can review your work by directing your attention to the Key Terms section at the end of your text.

absolute deprivation
affirmative action
discrimination
double jeopardy
dual labor market
environmental justice
glass ceiling
glass wall
informal economy
irregular or underground economy
institutional discrimination
relative deprivation
reverse discrimination
states' rights
total discrimination
underclass

V. TEST QUESTIONS

Multiple Choice Questions
Choose the correct answer from the choices provided.

1. Which of the following is defined as the conscious feeling of a negative discrepancy between legitimate expectations and present actualities?
a. reverse discrimination
b. total discrimination
c. relative deprivation
d. alienation

2. The denial of opportunities and equal rights to individuals and groups that results from the normal operations of a society is known as:
a. affirmative action.
b. institutional discrimination.
c. absolute deprivation.
d. all of the above.

3. According to Edna Bonacich, there are two realms of employment, one of which is populated by minorities working at menial jobs. The model that she uses to describe this is the:
a. dual labor market model.
b. last hired/first fired model.
c. informal economy model.
d. underground economy model.

4. The first anti-discrimination action at the executive level was known as:
a. affirmative action.
b. the Equal Employment Opportunities Commission.
c. the Fair Employment Practices Commission.
d. the Anti-Defamation League.

5. Researchers concluded that the underclass could qualify for _____ percent of jobs advertised in the Washington Post.
a. 5
b. 15
c. 35
d. 55

6. According to your text, which of the following groups has the highest median income?
a. Hispanic women
b. Hispanic men
c. African American women
d. African American men

7. White men, with a median income of $36,118 earn:

a. 89% more than Hispanic women.

b. almost 34% more than Black men.

c. more than White females.

d. all of the above.

8. The positive effort to recruit subordinate group members including women for jobs, promotions, and education opportunities is known as:

a. reverse discrimination.

b. affirmative action.

c. the Civil Rights Commission act.

d. scapegoating.

9. Rules requiring that only English be spoken in the workplace, even when not a business necessity, is an example of:

a. institutional discrimination.

b. prejudice.

c. scapegoating.

d. interpersonal discrimination.

10. Which of the following are regarded by the Glass Ceiling Commission to be glass ceiling barriers?

a. unfair recruitment practices

b. sex-based stereotyping

c. lack of day care facilities at the workplace

d. all of the above

True/False Questions

For each of the following statements, determine whether it is true or false. Write your answer in the space provided.

1. The informal economy makes up as much as 10-20 percent of all economic activity in the United States.

2. The groups of individuals who are most vocal and best organized against discrimination are usually in the worst economic and social situation.

3. Nondiscriminatory present practices of institutions can have negative effects because of prior intentionally biased practices.

4. Membership in the underclass in an intermittent condition.

5. Irish Catholics and Jewish Americans are less likely to be in certain positions of power than White Protestants, despite equal educational levels.

6. According to a 1973 Supreme Court ruling, attendance at an underfinanced school in a poor district constitutes a violation of equal protection.

7. In the 1978 Bakke case, the Supreme Court ruled that it was unconstitutional for universities to adopt flexible admissions programs that use race as a factor in decision making.

8. Affirmative action programs have caused a re-examination of height and weight policies.

9. Nepotism-based membership policies in some unions are examples of institutional discrimination.

10. The financial success of minorities leads to the elimination of prejudice.

Completion
Write in the word or words that best completes the following statements:

1. The subordinate status that is experienced by women of color is known as _____ _____.

2. The secondary labor market affecting many members of racial and ethnic minorities is known as the _____ _____.

3. Sociologist William Wilson states that black residents in inner-city ghetto neighborhoods _____ _____ the basic American values.

4. Current discrimination operating in the labor market and past discrimination is known as _____ _____.

5. The two main agents of social change that work toward reducing discrimination are _____ _____ and the _____ _____.

6. According to Stokely Carmichael and Charles Hamilton, covert acts collectively committed against an entire group are known as _____ _____.

7. The principle which holds that each state is sovereign in most of its affairs and has the right to order them without interference from the federal government is known as _____ _____.

8. The _____ case ruled that Whites may bring reverse discrimination claims against court-approved affirmative action plans.

9. The California _____ _____ Initiative prohibited any state programs that give preferences to women and minorities for college admission, employment, promotion, or government contracts.

10. Critics of affirmative action programs oppose specific hiring goals known as
_____.

Essay Questions

Answer the following questions to the best of your ability. Be sure to support your answers thoroughly.

1.William Julius Wilson argues that the Black residents of inner-city ghettoes want to work. What factors prevent this desire from being realized? What can be done to overcome these problems? Support your answer with facts from the text.

2. Schaefer indicates that there are two main agents of social change that work toward reducing discrimination: voluntary associations and federal government programs. In your opinion, which agent is most effective? Is it possible to reduce discrimination using only one agent or is it necessary for both to work together? Explain your answer and support your assertions going beyond the explanations offered in the text.

3. How would the functionalist and conflict perspectives explain the continuing existence of institutional discrimination? What solutions would each offer in dealing with such inequalities? In your opinion, which theory provides the best explanation and offers the best solutions? In your answer, be certain to support your assertions.

CHAPTER 4

Immigration and the United States

I. LEARNING OBJECTIVES

1. To learn about the history of immigration in the United States.
2. To understand the evolution of laws concerning immigration to the United States.
3. To question common stereotypes about immigrants.
4. To explore the distinction between legal and illegal immigration, and the roles that immigrants play in the U.S. economy.

II. CHAPTER OVERVIEW

The United States has always been largely populated by immigrants and their descendants. In this chapter, Schaefer shows us how immigrants have been treated both historically and currently in the United States, under the law and in civil society. Though immigration benefits the United States in many ways, there are many negative stereotypes of immigrants.

A. Early Immigration. In this section you are introduced to some of the early immigration policies of the United States. Specifically, the anti-Catholic and anti-Chinese movements are examples of how immigration rates and policies affect each other.
1. During the colonial period, what was the American approach to immigration?
2. List the many ways that dominant White Americans reacted to the influx of Irish Catholic immigrants during the 1800s. What political movement grew out of anti-Irish prejudice?
3. What are some examples of the prejudice and discrimination that met Chinese immigrants? How does conflict theory explain the increase in anti-Chinese sentiment?

B. Restrictionist Sentiment Increases. This section discusses immigration policy from the early 1900s through the 1960s, explaining the impact of the national origins system and the 1965 Immigration and Naturalization Act.
1. What was the Gentlemen's Agreement? How did its enactment illustrate the perceived difference between "old" and "new" immigrants?
2. Explain the national origins system and how it shaped immigration policy. How were quotas used in this system and what were the problems with this?
3. How did the 1965 Immigration and Naturalization Act change immigration policy? Using figure 4.2., show some examples of how this act changed the composition of nationalities who were allowed to enter the United States.

C. Contemporary Concerns. While immigration policy in the United States has changed significantly over time, there are three main criticisms of the current system. This section explains how concerns about the brain drain, population growth, and illegal immigration affect the debate around immigration.

1. What is the brain drain? How do conflict theorists view this phenomenon and why?
2. How is population growth affected by immigration?
3. What are some common concerns about illegal immigrants? How did the Immigration Reform and Control Act of 1986 address these concerns? What were the effects of its enactment?

D. The Economic Impact of Immigration. Economic reasons are often used as arguments against immigration. Despite findings that show positive economic effects of immigration, many people still hold negative stereotypes, as illustrated by the 1994 vote on Proposition 187 in California.
1. List some examples from the text that contradict the common negative perceptions about immigrants. What are the general conclusions we can draw from these studies?
2. Economically, how are states affected differently from the federal government by immigrants? What are some states doing to address this discrepancy?
3. What are the two opposing arguments on the issue of immigrants' remittances to their home countries?

E. Refugees. One group of immigrants that is unique in several ways are refugees. This section focuses on the United States' policy towards refugees, using Haitians as a recent example.
1. How is the situation of refugees different from that of other immigrants? What is the United States policy towards refugees in general?
2. How did both the Bush and Clinton administrations treat the situation of Haitian refugees? What are the criticisms of this policy?

III. CRITICAL THINKING QUESTIONS

1. Briefly explain the policies and attitudes that shaped the anti-Catholic and anti-Chinese movements. What similarities do you see between these phenomena and more recent examples, such as the passing of Proposition 187 or the treatment of Haitian refugees? Discuss how scapegoat theory can be used to explain such occurrences.

2. In this chapter, Schaefer discusses three popular concerns about immigration: the brain drain, population growth, and illegal immigration. Which of these three do you see as most legitimate? Why? Be sure to include why you think the other two are not as significant.

IV. KEY TERMS

Listed below are some of the key terms introduced in Chapter 4. After having read the chapter and completed the overview on the previous pages, check your comprehension of these terms by writing down the definitions in the space provided in your own words. You can review your work by directing your attention to the Key Terms section at the end of your text.

brain drain
nativism
refugees
remittances
sinophobes

xenophobia

V. TEST QUESTIONS

Multiple Choice Questions
Choose the correct answer from the choices provided.
1. Approximately what percentage of immigrants to the United States eventually return to their home countries?
a. 50 %
b. 72%
c. 35%
d. 10 %

2. The term nativism refers to:
a. respect towards native Americans.
b. beliefs and policies favoring native-born citizens over immigrants.
c. preference for one's native country over the new host country.
d. fear of strangers or foreigners.

3. What factor caused anti-Chinese sentiment to be more intense than anti-Irish feelings had been just a generation earlier?
a. poor economy
b. language barrier
c. their use as strikebreakers
d. racism

4. A concern about immigration policy which focuses on the immigration to the United States of skilled workers, professionals, and technicians is:
a. illegal immigration.
b. population growth.
c. the brain drain.
d. none of the above.

5. The only real way to lessen illegal immigration is to:
a. discourage employment opportunities.
b. increase effective policing at the borders.
c. restrict legal immigration further.
d. discourage multiculturalism.

6. A 1997 National Research Council report and a 1998 Cato Institute and National Immigration Reform report concluded that the economic impact of immigrants is:
a. uniformly positive.
b. uniformly negative.
c. positive overall, but negative in some regions.
d. negative overall, but positive in some regions.

7. Which group of refugees has NOT been allowed to enter the United States in greater numbers than policy would normally allow?
a. Hungarians
b. Haitians
c. Cubans
d. Southeast Asians

8. The most important of the social forces behind emigration are:
a. religious bigotries.
b. economic expectations.
c. dislike of new regimes.
d. wanting to reunite families.

9. Chinese workers were in great demand during the 1860s for the strenuous work on
a. the railroads.
b. the steel mills.
c. the mines.
d. none of the above.

10. Due largely to the national origins system, by the end of the 1920s, annual immigration had dropped to _____ of its pre-World War I level.
a. one-half
b. one-third
c. one-fourth
d. two-thirds

True/False Questions
For each of the following statements, determine whether it is true or false. Write your answer in the space provided.

1. Concerns about immigration are something new.

2. Irish Americans opposed freeing the slaves for fear of loss of job availability.

3. The quotas that were part of the national origins systems of immigration helped to relieve the backlog of people trying to enter the United States.

4. The effects of immigration on population are evenly distributed across the United States.

5. Despite common perceptions, immigration has had only a very slight impact on the employment opportunities of longtime U.S. citizens.

6. Remittances are monies that immigrants bring with them to the United States.

7. Nations smaller than the United States, such as Iran and Zaire, tend to admit many fewer refugees.

8. People fleeing their home countries to escape poverty do not fit the official definition of refugees.

9. After he took office, Clinton significantly altered the policy towards Haitian refugees enacted by the Bush administration.

10. Immigration was strictly regulated throughout much of the 1800s and naturalization was difficult.

Completion
Write in the word or words that best completes the following statements:

1. _____ _____ and _____ _____
_____ were two prominent Americans who encouraged prejudice against Irish Catholics.

2. People who fear anything associated with China are known as _____.

3. One effect of the 1965 Immigration and Naturalization Act is that _____ and _____ _____ now make up about 80 percent of those allowed to immigrate to the United States.

4. The Immigration Reform and Control Act of 1986 made the hiring of _____ illegal for the first time.

5. The State of California spends _____ dollars on illegal immigrants' education, health care and other services, but these immigrants generate _____ dollars a year in taxes.

6. The paradoxical situation of having a strong economy yet using economic arguments against immigration indicates that factors such as _____ and _____ tensions must be important factors in explaining current attitudes towards immigration.

7. _____ are people living outside of their native country for fear of religious or political persecution.

8. In the 1850s nativism became a political movement and party members became known as the
_____ _____.

9. _____ _____, founder of the American Federation of Labor, consistently opposed the inclusion of Chinese workers into the union.

10. While undocumented aliens are in the United States from throughout the world, Mexicans account for approximately _____ percent of the total.

Essay Questions

Answer the following questions to the best of your ability. Be sure to support your answers thoroughly.

1. Economic arguments are often used against immigration even though studies tend to show many positive contributions of immigrants. Explain how a conflict theorist and a functionalist would view the use of these arguments. Which perspective do you think makes the most sense? Be sure to defend your arguments thoroughly using examples from the text.

2. Refugees are seen as a unique type of immigrant. While many have been admitted to the United States, large numbers of refugees are denied entry. According to the text, what has been the experience of Haitian refugees attempting to immigrate to this country? What are the arguments for and against their admission? In your opinion, why has policy towards these refugees come to be the way it is? In your explanation, be sure to incorporate theories and definitions discussed in the text thus far. What do you think the U.S. approach towards Haitian refugees should be? Why?

3. Immigration policy in the United States has gone through many changes over time. Briefly explain some of the major phases of immigration and policy as discussed in the text. What factors are seen as problems or concerns now which have not been issues in the past? What concerns have been constant? Considering our current situation, what do you think immigration policy should be? What would be the arguments against your position? Be sure to address these concerns as you defend your position.

CHAPTER 5

Ethnicity and Religion

I. LEARNING OBJECTIVES

1. To understand how religion and ethnicity contribute to defining identity.
2. To understand the different sociological perspectives regarding the origins and functions of ethnicity in the United States.
3. To understand the formation of Whiteness as an identity, and the experiences of White ethnics in the United States.
4. To understand how race, religion, ethnicity, and class influence people's life chances.
5. To understand the religious diversity in the United States.

II. CHAPTER OVERVIEW

The discussion in this chapter focuses on the continuing (and increasing) significance of religion and ethnicity in the United States. Issues of Whiteness and White ethnics are examined as well as the interconnectedness of race, ethnicity, religion and class. Furthermore, this chapter explores the issue of life chances and how all of these factors alter one's ability to assimilate and thus succeed with regard to dominant cultural standards.

A. Ethnic Diversity. This section provides examples of ethnic diversity in the United States.
1. What is the largest ancestral group in the United States? Give an example of how members of this group maintain their ethnic tradition.
2. Provide an example from your own community or home town that is representative of the ethnic diversity of the United States. How do people in your community or home town go about maintaining their ethnic diversity?

B. Why Don't We Study Whiteness? This section explores the racial formation of Whiteness and the reasons for its comparative neglect as a topic of study.
1. Have the people classified White in contemporary U.S. society always been classified as White? Why do White people tend not to think about their own racial formation?

C. Religious Pluralism. This section provides an overview of religious diversity in the United States. It also addresses distortions in the media's depiction of the daily roles of religion.
1. What is the definition of denomination? What is the largest denomination in the United States?
2. The text states that religion in the United States is an ever-changing social phenomenon. Why do you think this is so? What social theory can you use to explain this?

D. The Rediscovery of Ethnicity. This section provides an overview of the functions of ethnic identity in the United States. In addition, the reasons for increasing ethnic awareness are discussed.

1. Why have sociologists viewed the persistence of ethnicity as dysfunctional? Which sociological theory can be used to explain this assertion?
2. What is Hansen's principle of third generation interest?
3. What is symbolic ethnicity? How might ethnic identity be compatible with assimilation?

E. The Price Paid by White Ethnics. This section discusses the negative attitudes of middle-class people toward White ethnics, and the stereotype of the White ethnic as the "typical bigot."
1. According to Michael Lerner, what is respectable bigotry? Can you cite examples of this in your own life experience?
2. According to the text, what are some of the reasons for the antagonism of White ethnics toward African Americans?

F. Case Example: The Italian Americans. This section provides insight into the obstacles faced by White ethnics in the United States through an overview of the Italian American experience.
1. What often-cited stereotype of Italian Americans is an example of respectable bigotry? According to the text, to what is the persistence of such a stereotype attributable?
2. What factors do you think contribute to the decline in ethnic identity for Italian Americans?

G. Ethnicity, Religion, and Social Class. This section discusses how the factors of race, religion, ethnicity, and class combine to influence one's life chances.
1. According to sociologist Max Weber, what are life chances? What factors affect the level of life chances one may experience?
2. It is often implied that religion and ethnicity are synonymous. While they may reinforce each other, how do they operate independently?
3. According to sociologist Milton Gordon, what does the term ethclass denote?

H. Religion in the United States. This section explores the diversity among the major Christian religions in the United States.
1. What is civil religion? What role does it play in reducing religious conflicts in the United States?
2. How can the history of the struggle within the Catholic church be characterized? What factors do you think lead to the outcome of this struggle?
3. What are secessionist minorities? Cite an example of a secessionist minority not offered in your text.

I. Limits of Religious Freedom: The Amish. This section discusses the limits of religious tolerance in the U.S. by exploring the experiences of the Amish.
1. How does Amish custom collide with U.S. law?

III. CRITICAL THINKING QUESTIONS

1. Considering your own identity, which factor is most important to you: race, religion, ethnicity or class? Which aspect of your identity limits your life chances the most? Which provides you with the greatest number of life chances? Explain your answer.

2. Why does the examination of "minority groups" generally not bring to mind the experience of White ethnics? In what ways are the obstacles faced by White ethnics similar to those faced by members of non-White ethnic groups? In what ways are they different? Explain your answer.

IV. KEY TERMS

Listed below are some of the key terms introduced in Chapter 5. After having read the chapter and completed the overview on the previous pages, check your comprehension of these terms by writing down the definitions in the space provided in your own words. You can review your work by directing your attention to the Key Terms section at the end of your text.

civil religion
creationists
denomination
ethclass
ethnicity paradox
life chances
principle of third-generation interest
respectable bigotry
secessionist minority
symbolic ethnicity

V. TEST QUESTIONS

Multiple Choice Questions
Choose the correct answer from the choices provided.

1. Which of the following represent the largest ancestral group in the United States?
a. Irish
b. Italian
c. German
d. English

2. How many religious bodies are represented in the United States today?
a. 10,000
b. 1,500
c. 500
d. 100

3. According to sociologist Herbert Gans, eating ethnic food, acknowledging ceremonial holidays, and supporting specific political issues are examples of:
a. religiosity.
b. assimilation.
c. ethnicity paradox.
d. symbolic ethnicity.

4. An important component of respectable bigotry is:
a. racism.
b. ethnic prejudice.
c. sexism.
d. class prejudice.

5. Many Italians during the early years of mass immigration received their jobs through an ethnic labor contractor known as the:
a. mezzogiorno.
b. padrone.
c. compatriot.
d. ACLU.

6. Which of the following has NOT been an issue in conflicts between Amish custom and mainstream U.S. practice:
a. compulsory school attendance.
b. child labor.
c. zoning laws.
d. Social Security and Workers' Compensation.

7. Perhaps the most prominent subgroup in the Roman Catholic church is the:
a. Hispanics.
b. Italians.
c. Irish.
d. Polish.

8. The 1962 Supreme Court decision that disallowed an allegedly non-denominational prayer drafted for use in the New York public schools was the case of:
a. *Yoder v. Wisconsin.*
b. *Edwards v. Aguillard.*
c. *Engel v. Vitale.*
d. *Smith v. Wesson.*

9. Which of the following is NOT an example of a liberal theological camp?
a. Methodists
b. Disciples of Christ
c. Congregationalists
d. Episcopalians

10. Which of the following is an example of a conservative theological camp?
a. Presbyterians
b. Congregationalists
c. Missouri Synod Lutherans
d. American Baptists

True/False Questions

For each of the following statements, determine whether it is true or false. Write your answer in the space provided.

1. There are more people in the Untied States with Irish ancestry today than there are people in Ireland.

2. While racial segregation can still be found in workplaces and educational institutions, it is hardly present in the churches of the United States.

3. Americans are turning to religion with the zeal of new converts.

4. The persistence of ethnic consciousness depends on foreign birth, a distinctive language, or a unique way of life.

5. According to sociologist Andrew Greeley, White ethnics are the "vanguard of conservatism."

6. For a small segment of Italian immigrants, entering and leading criminal activity was an aspect of assimilation.

7. Studies of contemporary religious involvement find that variations by ethnic background continue to emerge in the Roman Catholic church.

8. The Roman Catholic church has been a significant assimilating force.

9. Secessionist minorities reject assimilation but embrace cultural pluralism.

10. Recent surveys demonstrate that ethnicity is more significant in predicting attitude formation than religion.

Completion

Write in the word or words that best completes the following statements:

1. A large, organized religion not officially linked with the state or government is known as a _____.

2. In 1995, women made up _____ percent of clergy in the United States.

3. The ethnicity embraced today by English-speaking Whites is typically _____.

4. Jokes about Italians being connected to the Mafia are examples of _____ _____.

5. The dominant religion of Italian Americans is _____ _____.

6. The term _____ denotes the importance of both social class and ethnicity in determining one's social behavior and life chances.

7. The religious dimension in American life that merges the state with sacred beliefs is known as _____ _____.

8. Using survey data collected in 1963 and 1972, sociologist Andrew Greely concluded that, _____ was a stronger predictor of attitudes and beliefs than _____.

9. According to the text, religion becomes a mechanism for signaling _____ _____.

10. According to recent survey data, the Christian faith that has the highest proportion of affluent members is _____.

Essay Questions

Answer the following questions to the best of your ability. Be sure to support your answers thoroughly.

1. Which sociological perspective best explains the ethnicity paradox? In your opinion, does maintaining one's ethnic identity help or hinder one's ability to succeed in the United States? In your answer, be certain to incorporate the sociological perspective that best supports your assertions. In addition, provide evidence for your answer using examples from the text.

2. Hansen discusses the principle of third generation interest. What factors do you think lead to this principle? Incorporate concepts such as assimilation, life chances and pluralism into your answer. Do you think the existence of this principle increases or decreases the life chances of ethnic groups? Provide an example and support your answer.

3. The text says that there is an ethnic revival underway in the United States. Do you see evidence of this ethnic revival? If so, what factors to you feel have led to such a revival? If not, what factors do you think prevent it? Will an ethnic revival help or hinder minority and majority relations in the United States? Be certain to explain your answer and support your assertions thoroughly.

CHAPTER 6

The Native Americans

I. LEARNING OBJECTIVES

1. To learn about historical interactions between Europeans and Native Americans.
2. To learn about the history of legislation targeting Native Americans.
3. To understand how federal policies affect life on reservations.
4. To learn about pan-Indianism and how Native Americans today address issues of economic development, education, health care, religion, and the environment.

II. CHAPTER OVERVIEW

Focusing on the experience of Native Americans in the United States, this chapter discusses the history of their subordination by Europeans. Schaefer explains the development of policy towards Native Americans, which usually focused on relocation and assimilation. This chapter also explains the growth of pan-Indianism which serves to unite the many diverse native cultures in addressing issues which affect them collectively.

A. Early European Contacts. This section discusses some of the first impressions Europeans had of Native Americans and the results of the initial contacts between these groups.
1. What are the dangers of using the term *Indian cultures*?
2. What caused the decrease in Native American populations after European contact? Who bears responsibility?

B. Treaties and Warfare. During the nineteenth century, the United States continued its colonial-period policy towards Native Americans, which favored the interests of Whites. The case of the Sioux illustrates the harsh effects of these policies.
1. What was the goal of the Indian Removal Act of 1830? What effects did its passing have on both Native Americans and Whites?
2. Why was the Great Sioux Reservation broken up? How did this affect life for the Sioux?
3. What was the Ghost Dance, and why do scholars consider it a millenarian movement? How would a functionalist view this phenomenon?

C. Ruling the Native Americans. The federal government used legislation in addition to warfare to limit the options for Native Americans. This section discusses the Allotment Act and the Reorganization Act, explaining the goals of the United States in implementing them and how they influenced life for Native Americans.

1. Drawing on the text, compare the Allotment Act and the Reorganization Act on the points listed below:

	Allotment Act	Reorganization Act
Government goals		
Short-term effects		
Long-term effects		

2. Explain how these acts illustrate the federal government's desire to assimilate the Native Americans into White society.

D. Reservation Life and Federal Policies. While the federal government has historically maintained control over much of Native American life through such agencies as the Bureau of Indian Affairs, steps are now being taken to reduce government involvement and increase Native American autonomy. This section explains how legal claims, the Termination Act, and Employment Assistance Program work towards this goal, though with serious problems.
1. How did the government use setoffs when a land claim was found in Native Americans' favor? What were the problems with this system?
2. Do Native Americans prefer to recover their land, or receive financial compensation? Why do you think this is?
3. What were the original good intentions behind the Termination Act? What were the consequences of the Act after it passed in 1953?
4. What were the goals of the Employment Assistance Program? What are some of the intended and unintended effects it has had on life for Native Americans?

E. Pan-Indianism. This section discusses the more recent phenomenon of pan-Indianism, where different tribes unite to fight towards common goals. Organizations such as the National Congress of American Indians and the American Indian Movement range from moderate to radical and participate in different protests to improve the situation of Native Americans.
1. What inspired the *fish-ins*? What did they accomplish?
2. What were the demands of the members of the San Francisco Indian Center when they seized Alcatraz Island in 1969? What were the outcomes of the protest, both positive and negative?
3. What are some examples of more recent protests by pan-Indian groups? How do these illustrate the strengths and weaknesses of the pan-Indian movement?

F. Native Americans Today. While most of this chapter has focused on the history of Native Americans' interactions with Whites and the United States government, in this section Schaefer discusses the contemporary situation of Native Americans in the specific areas of economic development, education, health care, religion, and the environment.
1. Economically, how do tourism, government positions, and the gambling industry work both to the advantage and detriment of Native Americans?
2. How might we begin to address the extreme poverty that persists on reservations?
3. Why are the terms *kickout* or *pushout* more appropriate than *dropout* when referring to native American children who leave the school system.

4. What are some of the factors that negatively affect the quality of education for Native American students? Is the situation changing at all? How?

5. How are problems encountered by Native American college students similar to those of Native American children in elementary and high schools? How are these issues being addressed for Native Americans trying to earn a college degree?

6. What are some of the factors that contribute to poor health care for Native Americans? Keep in mind public services, structural barriers, cultural differences, and other related problems.

7. What are the barriers to freedom of religious expression for Native Americans and how are they being fought by native groups?

8. How does the term *environmental justice* relate to Native American concerns about the treatment of reservation lands? How do ecologists and sportsmen contest Native American ideas about environmental justice?

III. CRITICAL THINKING QUESTIONS

1. Chapter 6 discusses many examples of Native American protest through the pan-Indian movement, both successful and unsuccessful. Using specific examples, why do you think some of these protests were more successful than others? Considering these experiences, how might Native Americans best address their contemporary concerns? Explain why you think so.

2. Overall, do you think the situation of Native Americans in general is improving? Why or why not? Use specific examples from the text to defend your position.

IV. KEY TERMS

Listed below are some of the key terms introduced in Chapter 6. After having read the chapter and completed the overview on the previous pages, check your comprehension of these terms by writing down the definitions in the space provided in your own words. You can review your work by directing your attention to the Key Terms section at the end of your text.

crossover effect
environmental justice
fish-ins
internal colonialism
kickouts or pushouts
millenarian movements
pan-Indianism
powwows
setoffs
world systems theory

V. TEST QUESTIONS

Multiple Choice Questions
Choose the correct answer from the choices provided.

1. What does the term "American Indians" illustrate about the Europeans who first arrived in North America?
a.. They wanted to distinguish Native Americans from the West Indians of the Caribbean.
b.. They wanted to distinguish Native Americans from Asians.
c. The Native Americans reminded them a lot of East Indians.
d. They were confused about where they landed, believing they were in Asia.

2. Which of these was NOT a result of the Indian Removal Act of 1830?
a. Eastern tribes were forced to migrate across the Mississippi River.
b. A devastating massacre occurred at Wounded Knee.
c. Tribal lands were annexed for White settlement.
d. The movement was called the Trail of Tears.

3. Although the Reorganization Act recognized the diversity of tribes and the importance of tribal identity, its main goal was:
a. assimilation.
b. to make negotiations between tribes and the government easier.
c. to increase the power of the Bureau of Indian Affairs.
d. none of the above.

4. Which of the following is an example of services the Termination Act defined as "special" even though they fulfilled treaty obligations?
a. road equipment.
b. medical care.
c. college scholarships.
d. all of the above.

5. Founded in 1944, the _____ was the first national organization representing Native Americans.
a. Bureau of Indian Affairs
b. American Indian Movement
c. National Congress of American Indians
d. Iroquois League of Nations

6. More recent protest efforts of the American Indian Movement include:
a. objecting to spearfishing.
b. strategically occupying non-reservation land on a regular basis.
c. demanding the imprisonment of Leonard Peltier.
d. protesting the use of Native Americans as mascots for sports teams.

7. Two important sources of revenue and employment on reservations are:
a. tourism and gambling.
b. selling crafts and doing farm work.
c. government work and the lumber industry.
d. educating curious Whites on Native American spirituality and running powwows.

8. When referring to Native American children who quit school, the terms *kickout* or *pushout* are more appropriate than *dropout* because:
a. these children are usually forced to leave by racist White children.
b. the teachers actually kick them out of the classroom for misbehavior.
c. it illustrates that they left due to a hostile environment rather than individual shortcomings.
d. both a and b.

9. Which of these is NOT a problem in education for Native Americans?
a. language barriers
b. underfinancing
c. underenrollment
d. none of the above

10. A group formed in 1976 which continues to help Native Americans with certain environmental issues is the:
a. American Indian Environmental Council.
b. Council of Energy Resource Tribes.
c. Bureau of Indian Affairs.
d. Greenpeace.

True/False Questions
For each of the following statements, determine whether it is true or false. Write your answer in the space provided.

1. It is estimated that the population of Native Americans north of the Rio Grande was 10 million in 1500 but fell to 250,000 by 1900.

2. The Battle of Little Big Horn in 1876 was the last great Sioux victory.

3. The bureau of Indian Affairs and Native American Groups disagree about whether federal involvement in "Indian business' should be reduced.

4. The Employment Assistance Program was designed to help young Native Americans find jobs by relocating them to urban areas.

5. Fish-ins were protests involving strikes at fisheries where Native Americans worked.

6. Tim Giago feels that naming athletic teams after Native Americans honors their role in U.S. history.

7. Overall, Native Americans agree that gambling on reservations is beneficial and helpful to those living on reservations.

8. Although it is considered an illegal drug, it is now legal for Native Americans to use peyote for religious purposes.

9. For Native Americans, environmental issues are usually separate from land dispute cases.

10. As the situation of Native Americans continues to improve, the gap between their quality of life and that of other Americans is rapidly shrinking.

Completion
Write in the word or words that best completes the following statements:

1. According to the 1990 census, there are about _____ million Native Americans, and of these _____ percent live on reservations.

2. The _____ _____, which originally intended to make tribal members into landowners, eventually caused Native Americans to lose most of the land they had owned previously.

3. In land claim settlements, _____ are deductions from the money owed Native Americans that are equal to the federal services provided to the tribe.

4. _____ refers to social movement which unite several tribes in a common identity.

5. _____ _____ is the treatment of subordinate peoples like colonial subjects by those in power.

6. Nationally, Native American family incomes are typically _____ percent lower than those of the total population.

7. Official figures for unemployment rates on reservations range from _____ percent to _____ percent.

8. The _____ _____ refers to the drop in test scores of Native American children if the tests assume a lifelong familiarity of English.

9. Native Americans are now trying to strengthen the _____ _____ _____ _____ Act of 1978, which is supposed to ensure their freedom of religion.

10. The Ghost Dance was an example of a _____ _____.

Essay Questions

Answer the following questions to the best of your ability. Be sure to support your answers thoroughly.

1. The many acts discussed in Chapter 6 illustrate the federal government's paternalism towards Native Americans and a desire to have them assimilate, despite most of these acts having grown out of good intentions. Considering the issues facing Native Americans today, do you think that the government's approach has largely changed or remained the same? Why? Compare specific acts and responses to contemporary concerns in your answer.

2. The concepts of world systems theory and internal colonialism are used to discuss the subordination of Native Americans in the U.S. What do these concepts mean, and how can they be applied to the specific experience of Native Americans? Discuss this with particular reference to educational and economic problems. Consider the dilemmas of advocating mainstreaming vs. maintaining reservation life as possible solutions to these problems.

3. Pan-Indian movements have been useful for gaining many improvements for Native Americans. However, the situations of different tribes are unique in many ways, and should be addressed as such. Choose two examples of contemporary problems for Native Americans from the text and argue whether a pan-Indian or tribal approach would be a better approach. Explain your answer in detail and be sure to show why one approach is better than the other for each example.

CHAPTER 7

The Making of African Americans in a White America

I. LEARNING OBJECTIVES

1. To broaden your understanding of the history of African Americans from colonial times through the 1990s.
2. To understand the origins of slavery and its continuing impact on Black-White relations.
3. To understand the causes and nature of protest movements against racial inequality.
4. To explore the diversity of Black leaders' approaches to the problem of inequality.
5. To understand the role of religion in the struggle for racial equality in the United States.

II. CHAPTER OVERVIEW

This chapter provides an overview of the long history of slavery that continues to shape U.S. society and the lives of Black Americans today. It also discusses the history of Black resistance to racial oppression and inequality. The diverse strategies of African American leadership and the role of religion in Black struggles are considered.

A. Slavery. This section discusses the origins and the history of slavery in the United States. In providing this information it helps us to understand how past institutional practices continue to affect present-day White-Black relations.
1. What five central conditions provided the foundation for slavery in the United States? How did the slave codes help to maintain this foundation?
2. How did the slave codes affect the organization of family life and religious worship? What impact do you think this had on African American family life and religious worship today?
3. Who was involved in the abolitionist movement? Did all those who were opposed to slavery also oppose racial inequality?

B. Slavery's Aftermath. This section discusses some of the events immediately following Lincoln's issuing of the Emancipation Proclamation. It explores the political role of Blacks during Reconstruction and the subsequent efforts of Whites to limit Black participation.
1. What does the term Jim Crow mean? How do you think the past discrimination institutionalized in Jim Crow policies affects the life chances of African Americans today?
2. What was the White Primary? How did it affect the gains made during Reconstruction?

C. The Challenge of Black Leadership. This section outlines the various responses of Black American leaders to the institutionalization of White supremacy.
1. What approach did Booker T. Washington take toward eliminating White supremacy? What aspects of U.S. society made this approach effective at the time?

2. What was Du Bois' greatest objection to the politics of Booker T. Washington? What did Du Bois offer an as alternative? What is the talented tenth?
3. In your opinion, was Du Bois' approach more effective than that of Booker T. Washington? Which approach would be most effective in the approaching race relations today?

D. The Exodus Northward. This section outlines some of the key issues faced by Blacks as they migrated out of the South during the first half of the twentieth century.
1. What was the principal reason for Black migration out of the South? How was it similar to the immigration of Europeans to the United States?
2. What was the primary cause of the violent "red summer" of 1919? How would a conflict theorist explain this reaction?

E. Reemergence of Black Protest. This section outlines the factors that led to a new wave of protest against the persistent inequality experienced by African Americans in the middle of the twentieth century.
1. Why were mid-century protests surrounded by less violence than in 1919?
2. What is a *restrictive covenant*? How did these contracts contribute to the subordination of African Americans?
3. How would the functionalist perspective explain the maintenance of racial segregation policies in the armed forces? Is this explanation adequate? Why or why not?

F. The Civil Rights Movement. This section outlines some of the events in the movement for civil rights for African Americans. It focuses on efforts to eliminate *de jure* segregation in public schools as well as the use of civil disobedience in bus boycotts and other protests.
1. What is *de jure* segregation? How does it relate to the concept of assimilation? How was the situation of African Americans affected by the ending of this form of segregation with the Supreme court decision of *Linda Brown et al. v. Board of Education*?
2. How can the school segregation discussed in this section be related to the education of many African American school children today?
3. What is the belief behind civil disobedience? How was the use of such action different under Martin Luther King Jr.'s leadership?

G. Explaining Urban Violence. This section offers explanations for the increase in racial conflict experienced in the 1960s focusing on instances of urban violence.
1. What is the *riff raff* theory? How did it explain the role of rioters as well as the role of the dominant society in perpetuating or eliminating racial inequality?
2. What is *relative deprivation*? How can this concept be used to explain why violent Black protest increased in the United States?
3. What does the concept of *rising expectations* mean? How did this influence African Americans' expectations for equality of life chances?

H. Black Power. This section outlines the rise and fall of the Black Power Movement.
1. Schaefer says that cries of Black Power frightened Whites and offended many Blacks. Why? Does this happen during struggles for racial equality today?

2. What was the role of the Black Panther Party in the Black Power movement? Why did the leaders of this movement turn to more conventional means of struggling for racial equality?

I. The Religious Force. This section discusses the role of religion in the struggle for equality for African Americans in the United States.
1. How did religion both help and hinder the movement toward equality for Blacks in the United States? What role does religion play in this struggle today? Explain your answer.
2. What were the key ideas in the philosophy of Malcolm X? How did these ideas compare with those of previous Black political leaders?

III. CRITICAL THINKING QUESTIONS

1. What was the role of the media in the rising racial conflict of the 1960s? How does current media coverage influence national consciousness concerning race? Explain your answer.

2. Which Black leader, Booker T. Washington or W. E. B. Du Bois, would be most supported today? Explain your answer citing current struggles for racial equality.

IV. KEY TERMS

Listed below are some of the key terms introduced in Chapter 7. After having read the chapter and completed the overview on the previous pages, check your comprehension of these terms by writing down the definitions in the space provided in your own words. You can review your work by directing your attention to the Key Terms section at the end of your text.

abolitionists
civil disobedience
de jure segregation
ebonics
Jim Crow
relative deprivation
restrictive covenants
riff-raff theory
rising expectations
slave codes
White primary

V. TEST QUESTIONS

Multiple Choice Questions
Choose the correct answer from the choices provided.

1. Which of the following was NOT a common feature of slave codes?
a. A slave could not possess liquor.
b. Marriage between slaves was not legally recognized.

c. A slave could not gamble.

d. A slave could not testify in court against another slave.

2. The Supreme Court decision that state laws requiring "separate but equal" services for Blacks were a "reasonable" use of state government power was known as:

a. *Plessy v. Ferguson.*

b. *Williams v. Mississippi.*

c. *Brown v. Board of Education.*

d. the three-fifths compromise

3. Which of the following Black leader's approach to White supremacy is referred to as the politics of accommodation?

a. Frederick Douglas

b. W.E.B. Du Bois

c. Booker T. Washington

d. Sojourner Truth

4. According to the text, the most significant event for African Americans during the first half of the twentieth century was:

a. the acquisition of legal rights.

b. the demographic change in the distribution of Black people.

c. gaining the right to vote.

d. the enactment of Jim Crow policies.

5. The principle reason for Black migration out of the South during the first half of the twentieth century was:

a. for better economic opportunities.

b. to escape the oppression of slavery.

c. similar to the motivations of European immigrants.

d. both a and c.

6. The Supreme Court decision that challenged White primary elections endorsed in Jim Crow's formative period was known as:

a. *Plessy v. Ferguson.*

b. *Smith v. Allwright.*

c. *Linda Brown v. Board of Education.*

d. none of the above.

7. A private contract entered into by neighborhood property owners stipulating that property could not be sold or rented to certain minority groups was known as:

a. de facto segregation.

b. Jim Crow policy.

c. a restrictive covenant.

d. relative deprivation.

8. Those involved in the race riots in 1967 and 1968 included:
a. the uneducated.
b. the middle class.
c. the working class.
d. all of the above.

9. Who of the following was NOT and original organizer of the Black Panther Party?
a. Bobby Seale
b. Malcolm X
c. Huey Newton
d. All of the above were original organizers.

10. Which of the following denominations has the greatest following among Blacks?
a. Roman Catholic.
b. Muslim.
c. Methodist.
d. Baptist.

True/False Questions
For each of the following statements, determine whether it is true or false. Write your answer in the space provided.

1. Slave revolts and antislavery propaganda led to more restrictions on slaves and increased the intensity of oppression.

2. The Reconstruction Act of 1867 resulted in full participation in the political system on the part of Blacks.

3. The founding of the NAACP marked the beginning of conflict between White liberalism and Black militancy.

4. Currently, most African Americans live in the South.

5. Government programs were developed in the early twentieth century to confront the job discrimination experienced by African Americans in the growing ghettos of the North.

6. The end of World War II was followed by widespread racial violence.

7. Most violence between Whites and Blacks has been large-scale collective action.

8. The participants in race riots were mostly unemployed youth with criminal records.

9. The Black Power movement was born out of White violence.

10. Support of Black Power meant endorsing Black control of the political, economic, and social institutions in Black communities.

Completion
Write in the word or words that best completes the following statements:

1. _____, the distinctive dialect with a complex language structure found among Black Americans, exemplifies the African traditions that survive even a century after slavery.

2. Free Blacks and some sympathetic Whites developed the _____ _____ to bring escaping slaves to freedom in the North and Canada.

3. The movement, begun by W. E. B. Du Bois, that placed the responsibility for the problems facing African Americans on the shoulders of Whites was known as the _____ _____.

4. W.E.B. Du Bois advocated that the movement toward equality for Black Americans be led by the _____ _____.

5. The proposed protest by _____ _____ of 100,000 Blacks in a march on Washington in 1941 set a precedent for federal intervention in job discrimination.

6. _____ was founded in 1942 to fight discrimination with nonviolent direct action.

7. Segregation that results from children being assigned to schools specifically to maintain racially separate schools was known as _____ segregation.

8. The first incidence of nonviolent direct action used by Blacks to obtain rights that Whites already enjoyed was the _____ _____.

9. Stokely Carmichael of the Student Nonviolent Coordinating Committee (SNCC) argued that what Blacks needed in the struggle for equality was _____ _____.

10. Wali D. Fard first introduced Black Americans to the _____ religion in 1930.

Essay Questions
Answer the following questions to the best of your ability. Be sure to support your answers thoroughly.

1. How would a functionalist and a conflict theorist analyze the approaches taken by Black leaders in the 1950s and 1960s to end racial discrimination towards Black Americans? In your opinion, which perspective provides the best explanation? Using the perspective you have just discussed, what do you see are the most effective ways to address issues of racial inequality now present in the United States? Be certain to support your assertions.

2. What alternatives to the *riff-raff* theory can you offer to explain the urban riots that occurred in the 1960s? In your answer, be certain to explain how non-violent action still resulted in violent behavior. How might the understanding of the theory you offer help to prevent the outbreak of future riots related to struggles for racial equality? Support your answer using sociological perspectives as well as evidence from your text.

3. What factors led to the increased involvement of Black Americans in the political process during the era of Reconstruction? In what ways is it possible to increase the participation of African Americans in politics today? Will increasing the participation of members of this group improve their life chances? Why or why not? Support your answer using sociological concepts as well as information provided in your text.

CHAPTER 8

African Americans Today

I. LEARNING OBJECTIVES

1. To understand the impact of segregation on African American education.
2. To become familiar with the effects of low-income, prejudice, and discrimination on life for contemporary African Americans.
3. To learn about the current economic situation of African Americans.
4. To explore the strengths, weaknesses, and unique challenges of African American families.
5. To understand the causes and effects of residential segregation.
6. To become familiar with problems facing the African American community in areas such as criminal justice, health care, and politics.

II. CHAPTER OVERVIEW

The situation of African Americans has changed throughout the history of the United States. However, many problems persist. In this chapter, Schaefer focuses on education, the economy, family life, housing, crime and the judicial system, health care and politics, revealing challenges unique to African Americans.

A. Education. Education has been a concern for African Americans because it was forbidden during slavery and segregated after the Civil War. Issues of quality in education and the persistence of segregation remain.
1. Why is African American education of lower quality and lesser quantity? What can be done?
2. What is *de facto* segregation. Is busing a solution?
3. Why does tracking contribute to segregation within schools?
4. What causes fewer African Americans to obtain college degrees? What are some of the long term effects of this?

B. The Economic Picture. While the economic situation of African Americans has improved, there remains a large gap between them and Whites. We can explain this gap by looking at income and wealth, employment, and the difficulties facing African American business owners.
1. Explain the difference between income and wealth. How do these two categories show a gap between African Americans and Whites?
2. What are the unemployment rates for African Americans as compared to Whites? Why are these figures misleading?
3. What is the difference between set-asides and setoffs (discussed in Chapter 6)?
4. What challenges face Black business? According to Du Bois, what is a potential weakness of Black capitalism?

C. Family Life. The family is the first social institution with which we have direct contact. This section explores different arguments about the history, strengths and weaknesses of African American families?
1. How is the economic position of Black men related to the increase of female-headed households?
2. How has the African American family adapted to function in a hostile social environment?
3. What concerns are unique to the Black middle class? How have these been addressed?
4. What is William J. Wilson's argument about the relationship between class and race? What are the criticisms of his position?

D. Housing. Racism has affected the quality and availability of housing for African Americans. This section examines the factors that still contribute to residential segregation and unfair housing practices.
1. Why was housing one of the last areas to be addressed by civil rights legislation?
2. Why does residential segregation persist in the United States? How does *redlining* contribute to this?
3. How does the suburbanization of African Americans tend to recreate inner-city segregation? How do zoning laws affect this phenomenon?

E. Criminal Justice. The criminal justice system exemplifies very different experiences for African Americans and Whites. This section explores the causes and effects of these inequalities.
1. How would a conflict theorist explain the fact that Blacks account for 31 percent of arrests although they comprise only 12 percent of the population?
2. What is an example of differential justice, and how does it illustrate racism within the justice system?
3. What are the two main concerns of the African American community about crime?

F. Health Care. African Americans receive less health care than Whites, and they have more deaths from disease. This section links unequal health care to other kinds of discrimination.
1. How does sociologist Howard Waitzkin explain the medical condition of Black Americans?
2. How are African Americans represented in the health care system? How would this affect the medical resources of the community?
3. What is the relationship between *environmental justice* and the health of African Americans?

G. Politics. Although African Americans continue to be underrepresented in politics, they are gaining political influence on local, state and federal levels.
1. What are some encouraging signs that show an increase in African Americans' involvement in government leadership?
2. What is *gerrymandering* and how does it determine elections? How would a conflict theorist reply to critiques of this system?

III. CRITICAL THINKING QUESTIONS

1. Consider William J. Wilson's argument about the relationship between race and class for contemporary African Americans. Do you agree with his assertion? How does the situation of middle-class Blacks affect your argument?

2. Have African Americans made more gains in politics than in other areas or is this a misleading assumption? Explain your answer carefully using specific examples.

IV. KEY TERMS

Listed below are some of the key terms introduced in Chapter 8. After having read the chapter and completed the overview on the previous pages, check your comprehension of these terms by writing down the definitions in the space provided in your own words. You can review your work by directing your attention to the Key Terms section at the end of your text.

class
de facto segregation
differential justice
gerrymandering
income
redlining
set-asides
tracking
underemployment
victim discounting
victimization surveys
wealth
zoning laws

V. TEST QUESTIONS

Multiple Choice Questions
Choose the correct answer from the choices provided.

1. What are some deficiencies in the education of African Americans?
a. small classes and poor curricula
b. dilapidated facilities and insensitive teachers
c. apathetic administrators and poor transportation
d. small classes and poor transportation

2. The practice of placing students in specific curriculum groups on the basis of test scores and other criteria is known as:
a. guided learning.
b. redlining.
c. tracking.
d. differential education.

3. _____ refers to salaries, wages and other money received, while
_____ includes all of one's material assets.
a. Income, class
b. Wealth, income
c. Income, wealth
d. Class, wealth

4. Which of these is NOT considered a factor contributing to the unemployment of young African Americans?
a. They lack the desire to work.
b. They live in areas with depressed economies.
c. Illegal activities are more lucrative and readily available.
d. There is more competition in the labor force.

5. What is the most consistently documented strength of African American families?
a. a strong religious orientation.
b. an extended family household.
c. a strong work orientation.
d. flexible family roles.

6. The African American middle class:
a. encompasses at least 30 percent of the Black population.
b. are more likely than Whites to be first generation middle class.
c. have left the ghetto in search of better surroundings.
d. all of the above.

7. Zoning laws:
a. encourage residential integration.
b. forbid de facto housing segregation.
c. keep races separate in distinct residential zones.
d. sometimes encourage segregation in the suburbs.

8. When a crime is regarded as less significant because the victim is held to be less worthy, the phenomenon is referred to as:
a. victim discounting.
b. social apathy.
c. victim blaming.
d. redlining.

9. Blacks represent about _____ percent of practicing physicians.
a. 2.5
b. 5
c. 10
d. 25

10. The African American who ran for president in 1984 with a goal of creating a "Rainbow Coalition" was:
a. Tom Bradley.
b. Bobby Rush.
c. Jesse Jackson.
d. Maxine Waters.

True/False Questions
For each of the following statements, determine whether it is true or false. Write your answer in the space provided.

1. Head Start programs have allowed just as many African American children as White children to have pre-kindergarten schooling.

2. Racial incidents on predominantly White college campuses appear to be increasing.

3. Examining wealth reveals even greater disparity between Blacks and Whites than does income.

4. Set-asides refers to government incentives to White owned businesses.

5. Historically and in the present, the typical African American family is headed by a single mother.

6. After the civil rights movement, the quality of housing for African Americans improved to the same standards as Whites.

7. African Americans are 25 percent more likely to be victims of violent crime and 13 percent more likely to be victims of property crimes than are Whites.

8. Despite differences in many areas of social life, African Americans and Whites have the same life expectancy.

9. Jesse Jackson's visibility stems from his election to many public offices.

10. An increasing proportion of the Black population consists of immigrants.

Completion
Write in the word or words that best completes the following statements:

1. Although segregated schools are now illegal, due to residential patterns, _____ _____ segregation still persists.

2. In 1998, students at the historically Black colleges and universities accounted for about _____ percent of all Black college students.

3. If someone is working at a job for which she/he is overqualified or involuntarily working part time or temporarily, she/he is considered _____.

4. Sociologist _____ _____ _____ warned against viewing Black capitalism as a solution for all Black people.

5. Max Weber used the term _____ to refer to persons who share a similar level of wealth and income.

6. _____ refers to the practice of discrimination against people trying to purchase homes in minority or racially changing neighborhoods.

7. The fact that African Americans are dealt with more harshly by the criminal justice system than Whites is known as _____ _____.

8. Interviews of ordinary people carried out annually to reveal how much crime occurs are termed _____ _____.

9. The practice of creating voting districts in strange patterns for certain political outcomes in elections is known as _____.

10. The discrimination encountered in Patricia Williams's story (*Listen to Their Voices*) was an abuse of the _____ _____ Act.

Essay Questions

Answer the following questions to the best of your ability. Be sure to support your answers thoroughly.

1. Explain three of the many weaknesses in the educational system as outlined in Chapter 8. How do you think these problems would best be addressed? How are your suggestions different from what has been tried in the past? Defend your ideas with specific examples to explain how your solutions would be effective.

2. The debate concerning the relationship between race and class is ongoing as to whether they affect each other and which has a greater impact on an individual's life. Carefully illustrate arguments both for and against the idea that race and class are inseparable phenomena using examples found in the text, as well as your own examples. With which argument do you agree? Explain why the evidence for the other side falls short in your opinion.

3. Schaefer explains many aspects of social life that affect the lives of African Americans differently than Whites, and he shows how these areas tend to be connected. Choose two of the following areas (education, economic opportunity, family life, housing, criminal justice, health care or politics) and show how they affect each other. Which of the two areas you have chosen do you think would be a more effective area to institute change? Explain why you think so and how this would then affect the other areas for the better.

CHAPTER 9

Hispanic Americans

I. LEARNING OBJECTIVES

1. To learn about the diversity of the Latina/o or Hispanic population in the United States.
2. To understand the important elements of Hispanic identity.
3. To learn about the significance of language to Latina/o identity as well as the key components of the debates surrounding this issue.
4. To understand the significance of the *borderlands* to Mexicans and Mexican Americans as well as other Hispanic groups.
5. To understand the experiences of Cuban immigrants to the United States and the issues they face as they remain in this country.
6. To understand the diversity of experiences of Central and South American immigrants to the United States and the possibilities for future generations of these immigrants.

II. CHAPTER OVERVIEW

This chapter begins an examination of the diversity of Hispanic people residing in the United States. Specifically, it focuses on the importance of language to the various Hispanic cultures in the U. S. as well as the efforts that different immigrant groups have made to establish a sense of economic and cultural security. Finally, this chapter discusses the issues faced by the most recent Hispanic immigrants to this country: Central and South Americans.

A. Hispanic Identity. This section outlines some of the key factors Hispanics face in developing an Hispanic identity.
1. What is panethnicity? According to these section, are Hispanics developing a panethnic identity?
2. What are some of the issues that impact the ability of Latinas/os to develop a common identity? Is it necessary for such an identity to develop? Why or why not?

B. The Language Divide. This section discusses the importance of the Spanish language to maintaining the cultures of Hispanics. In addition, it addresses some of the key components to either side of the language debate.
1. According to this section, how do most Anglos view the Spanish language and those who speak Spanish? How would a conflict theorist explain this attitude?
2. How do the policies in the U.S. toward the use of the Spanish language impact Hispanics and their cultural identity and heritage?
3. What is the basis for the opposition of the U.S. English organization to bilingualism? What do critics of this movement say?

C. The Borderlands. This section introduces the concept of the *borderlands* and its significance to Mexicans and Mexican Americans as well as other Hispanic groups.

1. What are the borderlands? What is the significance of separate Mexican and U.S. cultures in the borderlands? Why is this so?

2. What are the *maquiladoras*? How do they affect the economy of the United States?

D. Cuban Americans. This section discusses the historical events that resulted in a large influx of Cubans to the United States. In addition, it discusses the influence that these immigrants have had on the United States, focusing on Miami.

1. Who are *Marielitos*? What does this term imply? What is its significance in the Cuban community today?

2. What factors resulted in the difficult transition of members of the third wave of immigration from Cuba to the United States? What is the status of this group today?

3. What has been the influence of Cubans on the economy of Miami? What is the general feeling of non-Cuban Americans toward this economic influence?

4. What is the relationship of Miami's Cuban Americans with other groups? How would a conflict theorist view this situation?

5. What factors influence the long-range prospects for Cubans in the United States? How does assimilation influence their prospects?

E. Central and South Americans. This section describes the complexity of experiences faced by the diverse populations that have immigrated to the United States from Central and South America.

1. What is the color gradient? How is it a reminder of the social construction of race?

2. Historians Ann Orlov and Reed Ueda conclude that "social relations among Central and South American ethnic groups in the United States defy generalization." What do they mean by this? Cite examples to illustrate your answer.

3. How does the immigration of Central and South Americans to the United States reflect brain drain? How does this affect their home countries?

4. What are the different possibilities for the future of Central and South Americans in the United States? Which possibility do you think to be the most likely? Why do you think this?

III. CRITICAL THINKING QUESTIONS

1. Language can have a strong connection to culture. In your own life, how do you see your native language reflecting your culture? How might your life change if you were no longer able or no longer permitted to speak your native language? Reflecting on this, how does this make you view the issues discussed in this chapter differently, if at all? Explain your answer.

2. This chapter mentions many of the ways Hispanic cultures have influenced life in the United States. Are these influences evidence of the acceptance of these different cultures or mere tokenism? Explain your answer.

IV. KEY TERMS

Listed below are some of the key terms introduced in Chapter 1. After having read the chapter and completed the overview on the previous pages, check your comprehension of these terms by writing down the definitions in the space provided in your own words. You can review your work by directing your attention to the Key Terms section at the end of your text.

bilingual education
bilingualism
borderlands
brain drain
color gradient
English immersion
maquiladoras
Marielitos
panethnicity
remittances (or migradollars)

V. TEST QUESTIONS

Multiple Choice Questions
Choose the correct answer from the choices provided.

1. The largest Hispanic population in the United States consists of:
a. Puerto Ricans.
b. Mexican Americans.
c. Latinos.
d. Cubans.

2. Efforts to speak two or more languages in schools or at work and to treat each language with equity are known as:
a. bilingualism.
b. biculturalism.
c. assimilation.
d. pluralism.

3. The 1970 U.S. Supreme Court ruled that *de jure* segregation of Mexican Americans was unconstitutional in:
a. schools.
b. voting.
c. housing.
d. employment.

4. Which sociological perspective would be most likely to emphasize that resistance to bilingual programs stems from the effort to assimilate members of subordinate groups, to restrict their political power, and maintain the cultural dominance of Anglos?
a. conflict
b. mainstreaming
c. functionalist
d. cultural assimilation

5. Foreign companies who establish operations in Mexico yet are exempt from Mexican taxes are known as:
a. Marielitos.
b. borderland operations.
c. migradollars.
d. maquiladoras.

6. According to the text, Cubans are third in numbers in the United States only to:
a. Chicanos and Latinos.
b. Mexican Americans and Puerto Ricans.
c. Mexicans and Haitians.
d. Mexican Americans and Brazilians.

7. The Cuban refugees of the third wave of migration to the United States are known as:
a. The Boat People.
b. Freedom Followers.
c. Maquiladoras.
d. Marielitos.

8. The latest wave of Cuban immigrants to the United States are known as:
a. Marielitos.
b. recien llegados.
c. maquiladoras.
d. refugees.

9. Which of the following terms is NOT a reflection of the color gradient of the nations of Central and South America?
a. mestizo Hondurans
b. mulatto Colombians
c. recien llegados
d. African Panamanians

10. Colombians who immigrated to the United States after World War 1 quickly assimilated because:
a. they were educated and middle class.
b. bilingual schools were not available.
c. English was learned on the job.
d. most moved to Mexican American neighborhoods.

True/False Questions

For each of the following statements, determine whether it is true or false. Write your answer in the space provided.

1. The majority of Hispanics in the United States refer to themselves by panethnic names.

2. English as a Second language programs tend to emphasize bilingual, but not bicultural, education.

3. English is the official language of the United States.

4. Efforts to pass a constitutional amendment making English an official language have failed in the U.S.

5. The borderlands along the border between Mexico and the United States hold little importance to Latinas/os other than Mexicans and Mexican Americans.

6. There have been three waves of immigration from Cuba to the United States.

7. The majority of Cuban Americans live in Miami.

8. Cuban immigrants feel they need to forget Spanish while establishing fluency in English as do other immigrant groups.

9. As a group, Central and South Americans experience high unemployment and are better educated than other Hispanics in the United States.

10. The immigration of Central and South Americans to the United States has resulted in a brain drain.

Completion

Write in the word or words that best complete the following statements:

1. The development of solidarity among ethnic subgroups is known as _____.

2. The Supreme Court decision that *de jure* segregation of Mexican Americans was unconstitutional is known as _____ v. _____ _____
_____ _____.

3. Proposition 227 abolishes _____ _____ in California.

4. Federal law requires bilingual or multilingual ballots in voting districts where at least _____ percent of the population belong to a single minority group.

5. The flow of money that Mexicans and other Hispanics created by sending part of their earnings back across the border to family members remaining in their native country is known as

_____ _____.

6. Foreign companies who establish operations in Mexico yet are exempt from Mexican taxes are known as _____.

7. The third major migration of Cubans to the U.S. occurred in what is termed the

_____ _____.

8. The Cuban refugees of the third major migration to the United States were given the name _____ by other Cubans.

9. The placement of people along a continuum from light to dark skin color rather than in distinct racial groupings by skin color is known as a _____ _____.

10. Immigration to the United States of skilled workers, professionals, and technicians is known as

_____ _____.

Essay Questions
Answer the following questions to the best of your ability. Be sure to support your answers thoroughly.

1. This chapter discusses various perspectives on the importance of bilingual education and the speaking of English in the United States. How would a functionalist and a conflict theorist view the push toward English as the "official" language of the United States? Which perspective best reflects your own opinion? In your discussion, be certain to include concepts such as assimilation, pluralism, marginality, ethnocentrism and other relevant concepts that you have learned in this and previous chapters. Be certain to support your answer thoroughly.

2. According to the text, what are the key factors that unify members of Hispanic cultures in the United States? What factors stand in the way of their ability to unify? In your opinion, is it necessary for different Hispanic cultures to unify? How might this help their place in the stratification system of the United States? How might it hinder their progress? Explain your answer supporting your assertions using information from the text.

3. How do issues of class prejudice enter into the ways in which different waves of Cuban immigrants relate? What other forms of bias do you see present? In your opinion, will the different waves of Cuban immigrants be able to overcome these prejudices on their own? In what ways do the biases present in the dominant culture of the United States perpetuate these prejudices? Explain your answer, supporting your assertions with concepts and other materials from the text.

CHAPTER 10

Mexican Americans and Puerto Ricans

I. LEARNING OBJECTIVES

1. To understand the similarities and differences between the experiences of Mexican Americans and Puerto Ricans in the United States.
2. To become familiar with the factors influencing the immigration of Mexicans to the United States.
3. To learn about the unique relationship between Puerto Rico and the United States and how this affects Puerto Ricans.
4. To be introduced to the situation of Mexican Americans and Puerto Ricans in the United States in regard to education, economic opportunities, family life, access to health care, involvement in politics, and religion.

II. CHAPTER OVERVIEW

As the two largest groups of Hispanics in the United States, Mexican Americans and Puerto Ricans share many similar experiences. However, both in the past and in the present, the situations of these groups also differ because of the different relationships the United States maintains with Mexico and Puerto Rico. In this chapter, Schaefer highlights these distinctions by explaining the United States' historical and contemporary economic and immigration policies with these countries. In addition to this international perspective, he discusses the current situation of these groups in the United States.

A. Mexican Americans. This section introduces the history of relationships between Mexicans and the United States, including conquest and migration. It also discusses the economic and political history and current status of Mexican Americans.
1. What were the results of the Mexican-American War?
2. What generalizations can be made about Mexican Americans in the nineteenth century? Explain the pattern of treatment they received during this time.
3. How have American corporations used Mexican workers? How would a conflict theorist explain why this occurs?
4. When has the U.S. encouraged Mexicans to immigrate as laborers and when has it restricted Mexican immigration? What were the repatriation, braceros and Operation Wetback programs?
5. What does the term La Raza mean? Why is this concept important to Mexican Americans?
6. What is the culture of poverty theory and how does it explain the persistence of poverty? What are the criticisms of this theory?
7. What are the findings of recent studies comparing Mexican and White American families?
8. Who was Cesar Chavez and what were his accomplishments?
9. What is Chicanismo and how is it related to the colonial model?
10. What are the goals of the Federal Alliance of Land Grants and the Mexican American Legal Defense and Education Fund, respectively?

B. Puerto Ricans. This section introduces the history of Puerto Rico's relationship with the United States, and discusses the impact of this relationship on the experiences and ambitions of Puerto Ricans.

1. What were the results of the Spanish-American War?
2. What factors have contributed to the migration of Puerto Ricans from the island to the mainland?
3. Who is considered a Neorican? How are they viewed by native Puerto Ricans?
4. What is neocolonialism? How does this concept illuminate the history of Puerto Rico?
5. What are the main respective arguments for independence, statehood, or maintaining the commonwealth? What does the outcome of the 1998 vote illustrate about where most Puerto Ricans stand on this issue?
6. Explain the difference between how Puerto Ricans and mainland Americans define racial categories. How might this affect Puerto Ricans moving to the mainland?
7. What is world systems theory, and how does it explain the economy of Puerto Rico?

C. The Contemporary Picture of Mexican Americans and Puerto Ricans. This section discusses and compares the current status and problems of Mexican Americans and Puerto Ricans in several areas of civil society.

1. Why is there a persistent gap between Hispanic and White American successes in education? How does tracking contribute to this?
2. How have some educational institutions responded to the social reality of *borderlands* and cross-border movement?
3. What is *familism* and what are some of its significant aspects? What does the author expect to be the future of this institution?
4. How does the health care for Hispanic Americans compare with that of other groups in America?
5. What is *curanderismo*, and is it a cause or effect of the relationship that Hispanics have with the health care system?
6. What kind of role has the Roman Catholic church historically played for Hispanics? Conversely, what role have Hispanics played in shaping the culture of the church?
7. What is pentecostalism and why is it attractive to many Latinas/os?

III. CRITICAL THINKING QUESTIONS

1. How have the wars of the nineteenth century shaped the current relationship between Mexico and Puerto Rico and the United States? What are some contemporary issues that reflect this history? Are there concerns that are unrelated to this legacy? Be specific as you explain your answer.

2. How do the current situations and predicaments of Mexican Americans and Puerto Ricans compare? To what extent has their common experience translated into political solidarity? What factors inhibit the development of a Hispanic panethnicity?

IV. KEY TERMS

Listed below are some of the key terms introduced in Chapter 10. After having read the chapter and completed the overview on the previous pages, check your comprehension of these terms by writing down the definitions in the space provided in your own words. You can review your work by directing your attention to the Key Terms section at the end of your text.

bracero
chicanismo
color gradient
culture of poverty
curanderismo
familism
La Raza
life chances
mojados
neocolonialism
Neoricans
Pentecostalism
repatriation
tracking
world systems theory

V. TEST QUESTIONS

Multiple Choice Questions
Choose the correct answer from the choices provided.

1. In the nineteenth century, many Mexicans became aliens in the United States by:
a. escaping from Mexico in search of better jobs.
b. living in areas annexed by the United States at the conclusion of the Mexican-American War.
c. living in the U.S. but refusing to become citizens.
d. wishing to maintain cultural integrity.

2. Why is immigration from Mexico unique?
a. It has been a continuous movement for most of this century.
b. Mexican immigrants can maintain close ties with their homeland.
c. There is a constant suspicion of illegality towards Mexican immigrants.
d. all of the above.

3. Which of these is NOT a factor contributing to the migration of Puerto Ricans to the mainland?
a. the economic pull away from the island
b. the availability of unrestricted travel
c. cheaper airfares
d. the desire to learn better English

4. According to the text, the FALN of Puerto Rico believed that the island should:
a. use violence to free itself from the United States.
b. become the fifty-first state of the Union.
c. remain a commonwealth.
d. campaign for independence through the ballot box.

5. Which of these has contributed to the increase in social isolation for Mexican Americans and Puerto Ricans in the educational system?
a. They have intentionally created their own system of private schools.
b. These students cannot interact with their White peers due to language barriers.
c. More and more, Hispanics are concentrated in large cities where minorities dominate.
d. all of the above.

6. Studies comparing Anglo families with Mexican American families in the same social class tend to find that:
a. Mexican Americans have a stronger work ethnic.
b. these groups have very different forms of family organization.
c. there is little difference between beliefs and about child rearing, family organization, or work ethics.
d. Anglo Americans take child rearing more seriously.

7. Successes of Cesar Chavez and the United Farm Workers include:
a. insuring good housing for migrant workers.
b. nearly eradicating alcoholism and malnutrition among migrant workers.
c. improving working conditions.
d. providing adequate education to migrant workers' children.

8. A possible negative effect of familism is:
a. it is hard to make friends when family is the constant focus.
b. the belief that one's family can do no wrong.
c. youth may not take advantage of opportunities that would remove them from the family.
d. everyone is always in each other's business.

9. Curanderismo refers to:
a. Hispanic folk medicine.
b. fright sickness.
c. pride and closeness in the family.
d. Puerto Ricans in New York.

10. The primary civil rights group for Mexican Americans and other Hispanics is the:
a. La Raza Unida.
b. Mexican-American Legal Defense and Education Fund.
c. United Farm Workers.
d. Alianza Federal de Mercedes.

True/False Questions

For each of the following statements, determine whether it is true or false. Write your answer in the space provided.

1. Since Puerto Rico is a commonwealth of the United States, its inhabitants are not considered U.S. citizens.

2. Ironically, there was a time when some Mexicans were being brought into the U.S. through the Bracero program, while others were being deported through Operation Wetback.

3. Neoricans are viewed with animosity by long-time residents of Puerto Rico.

4. Militant Puerto Rican nationalists attempted to assassinate President Truman in 1950.

5. Lack of motivation is the main barrier to academic achievement for Mexican immigrants.

6. Cesar Chavez founded the United Farm Workers union and had many successes with improving the working conditions for migrant workers.

7. Although the United States government has succeeded in attracting businesses to Puerto Rico, the island's economy still has many problems.

8. The importance of familism for Hispanics is expected to decline in the future.

9. Mexican Americans who are United States citizens can also be citizens of Mexico.

10. Most Hispanics are members of a Pentecostal church.

Completion

Write in the word or words that best completes the following statements:

1. The term _____ refers to the program of sending Mexicans back to Mexico in the 1930s.

2. Although it literally means "the people," _____ _____ connotes pride in Mexican American heritage.

3. In Puerto Rico, _____ percent of the inhabitants speak English, and _____ percent are bilingual.

4. The continuum of the _____ _____ allows for more fluid definitions of race in Puerto Rico which contrasts with how race is defined in the United States.

5. The _____ _____ _____ theory is another way of blaming the victim for social inequality.

6. The goals of UFW's _____ _____ , started in 1965, were improved working conditions and union recognition.

7. Corporations have been the focus of improvement for Puerto Rico's economy, and as a result, _____ has been ignored.

8. A _____ of Hispanics have no health insurance, which is much higher than the rate of uninsured Whites and Blacks.

9. _____ _____ _____ founded the Federal Alliance of Land Grants in 1963 with the goal of recovering lost land for Mexican Americans.

10. A type of evangelical Christianity, _____ is growing among Hispanics in the United States.

Essay Questions
Answer the following questions to the best of your ability. Be sure to support your answers thoroughly.

1. As discussed in Chapter 10, Puerto Ricans disagree about whether they should remain a commonwealth of the United States, become a state of the United States or become an independent nation. Considering what you have learned, which do you think is the best option for Puerto Ricans? Discuss areas such as the economy and cultural identity as you explain your answer. Also, be sure to illustrate why the other two options would be worse for Puerto Ricans than the one you have chosen.

2. How has the treatment of Mexican immigrants changed over time? What factors do you think are the most important in determining whether or not they are welcomed by the United States' government? How does this explain the current view of Mexican immigrants? Draw on specific concepts, theories, and examples from the text in your answer.

3. While Hispanics have great strengths in the areas of family life and religious involvement, they continue to lag behind White Americans in educational attainment, economic success, health care, and involvement in formal politics. Choose two of these last four categories of social life and explain why you think large gaps between the experiences of these groups persist. Where would it make the most sense to focus on solutions? Why? Can the strengths of the Hispanic community be used to address these problems? Why or why not?

CHAPTER 11

Asian Americans: Growth and Diversity

I. LEARNING OBJECTIVES

1. To understand the experience of Asian Americans in general and the experiences of Koreans, Filipinos, Asian Indians and refugees from Southeast Asia more specifically.
2. To explore the image of the "model minority" and how this stereotype impacts the life chances of Asian Americans.
3. To gain an awareness of the political efforts of different Asian American populations, as well as an understanding of some of the reasons for their lack of political participation.
4. To gain an awareness of the experiences of Filipino immigrants to the United States and the unique limitations that this group of Asian Americans face.
5. To learn about the issues faced by Asian Indian immigrants to the United States.
6. To understand the experiences of refugees and other immigrants from Southeast Asia and the current issues they face.
7. To learn of the ways in which Korean Americans have worked to move out of their subordinate status.
8. To gain an awareness of Hawaii and its people, understanding the factors that lead to its diversity as well as the issues that such diversity presents.

II. CHAPTER OVERVIEW

This chapter begins by exploring the image of Asian Americans as the "model minority" as well as their political activities. Although often viewed as a monolithic group, the population of Asian Americans is comprised of a great diversity of peoples and cultures. This chapter provides an introduction to the four larger groups—Filipino Americans, Asian Indians, Southeast Asian Americans, Korean Americans—and also to Hawaii and its people. The discussion focuses on the history of immigration for each group as well as the issues they currently face within the United States. The racial and ethnic pluralism of Hawaii is also discussed.

A. The "Model-Minority" Image Explored. This section examines the socioeconomic status of Asian Americans, and questions the "model-minority" view.
1. What is the concept of the model or ideal minority? How does this stereotype help to maintain the notion of the "American Dream"? How does it relate to the notion of "blaming the victim"?
2. What are some of the issues faced by Asian American students on college campuses? How are these issues exacerbated by racial harassment?
3. How does the glass ceiling influence the professional development of Asian Americans? How do their experiences compare with those of other subordinate groups?
4. What are middlemen minorities? What creates them? How do the occupational experiences of this group differ from the experiences of other racial and ethnic minorities?

5. What is the role of the *Yellow Peril* in increased violence against Asian Americans? How do media images of Asian Americans contribute to this problem?

B. Political Activity. This section discusses the political efforts of different Asian American populations, also explaining the relative lack of political participation among this group.
1. How have Asian Americans fought anti-immigrant attitudes? How has this political activity been similar to or different from the patterns of other immigrant groups?
2. What are some of the reasons that Chinese Americans have not been more active in politics? Why are they and other Asian Americans now being regarded as a future political force in the United States?
3. What must happen in order for Asian Americans to gain greater political success?

C. Diversity among Asian Americans. This section discusses the diverse backgrounds and profiles of the Asian American population.
1. How do Asian Americans vary by homeland and geographical distribution in the U.S.?

D. Filipino Americans. This section discusses the often overlooked experiences of Filipinos in the United States. In addition to focusing on the historical events of their immigration, this chapter also provides a brief overview of the condition of Filipinos in the U.S. today.
1. What were the four periods of Filipino immigration? How do these periods coincide with the immigration patterns of other groups discussed in this and previous chapters?
2. What is the economic situation of U.S.-born Filipinos? What factors lead to this economic condition? How does their capacity for economic development compare to other Asian American groups?
3. What are the reasons for the lack of formation of a significant Filipino social organization? How does this affect their visibility as a culture and a community in the United States?

E. Asian Indians. This section discusses the experiences of Asian Indian immigrants to the United States, focusing on historical factors as well as present-day issues.
1. In general, what is the role of religion in Asian Indian culture? How does it differ for immigrants versus those who remain in India?
2. What challenges to tradition are faced by Asian Indian families?
3. What reasons might Asian Indian young people have for agreeing to maintain the tradition of arranged marriages? How is this tradition being affected by the practices of the dominant U.S. culture?

F. Southeast Asian Americans. This section outlines the experiences of refugees and other immigrants from Southeast Asia. In addition, it addresses some of the concerns currently facing these groups.
1. What was the primary objection to Vietnamese immigration? How is this reaction similar to that received by other immigrant groups?
2. What is the *gook syndrome*? What was the role of the media in perpetuating this phenomenon?
3. What was the result of federal government efforts to disperse the refugees from Vietnam, Cambodia, and Laos? How is this related to the desire to maintain the culture of these immigrant groups?

G. Korean Americans. This section discusses the historical background of the Korean American experience. In addition, it addresses some of the current issues that Korean Americans face in the United States and how this culture works to address these issues.

1. How can the third wave of Korean immigration be related to the concept of brain drain discussed in previous chapters?

2. How are members of the *ilchomose* generation characterized? How does their experience compare with that of immigrants discussed in previous chapters, such as Cubans?

3. Why does Korean American women's participation in the labor force cause them to break cultural tradition? How complete is this move away from traditional cultural roles?

4. What is the role of the church in Korean American culture? How is this similar to the experience of other subordinate groups that you have read about in previous chapters?

H. Hawaii and Its People. This section explains the historical circumstances that resulted in Hawaiian ethnic diversity, and the issues this diversity presents.

1. Who are the AJAs? What is their role in Hawaiian culture?

2. Why does the racial consciousness of Hawaii differ from that on the mainland?

3. What is the economic status of native Hawaiians? What role do they see the U.S. occupation of Hawaii playing in their current economic condition?

III. CRITICAL THINKING QUESTIONS

1. The chapter discusses conflicts between members of different subordinate groups, such as Korean Americans and African Americans. What do you see as the source of this conflict? How does this conflict serve to perpetuate their subordinate status? Explain your answer.

2. What is wrong with the stereotype of Asian American students as "academic stars"? How does it affect how we view the actions of members of other subordinate groups? How can the problems faced by these students can be addressed? Explain your answer.

IV. KEY TERMS

Listed below are some of the key terms introduced in Chapter 11. After having read the chapter and completed the overview on the previous pages, check your comprehension of these terms by writing down the definitions in the space provided in your own words. You can review your work by directing your attention to the Key Terms section at the end of your text.

AJAs
gook syndrome
Haoles
ilchomose
kye
middlemen minorities
model or ideal minority
panethnicity
Viet Keiu

yellow peril

V. TEST QUESTIONS

Multiple Choice Questions
Choose the correct answer from the choices provided.

1. Which of the following is a characteristic of the ilchomose?
a. middle-aged
b. bilingual
c. professional
d. all of the above

2. The largest concentration of Korean Americans in the United States can be found in:
a. New York City.
b. Hawaii.
c. Los Angeles.
d. Chicago.

3. Which is the second largest Asian American group in the United States?
a. Chinese
b. Filipinos
c. Koreans
d. Southeast Asians

4. As of 1990, the state with the largest concentration of Asian Indians was:
a. New York.
b. Illinois.
c. California.
d. Florida.

5. The term sometimes used to refer to more than a million Vietnamese fleeing religious persecution in Indochina was the:
a. boat people.
b. Haoles.
c. AJAs.
d. Marielitos.

6. Hawaii was initially populated by which of the following people?
a. Japanese
b. Polynesians
c. Haoles
d. both b and c

7. Which of the following groups of people holds the top business positions in Hawaii?
a. Haoles
b. Koreans
c. Japanese Americans
d. Filipinos

8. Top positions in politics in Hawaii are occupied primarily by:
a. Whites.
b. Japanese.
c. Hawaiians.
d. Polynesians.

9. The effort to seek restoration and compensation for the native Hawaiian land that has been lost to Anglos over the last century is known as:
a. the restoration movement.
b. the prosovereignty movement.
c. the Haole movement.
d. the Polynesian restoration movement.

10. Which of the following is an issue faced by Asian American students on college campuses?
a. harassment
b. lack of Asian faculty and staff
c. alienation
d. all of the above

True/False Questions
For each of the following statements, determine whether it is true or false. Write your answer in the space provided.

1. Americans tend to lump Korean Americans together with other Asian groups.

2. Due to economic pressures, the majority of first generation immigrant Korean couples have discarded traditional gender divisions in daily life.

3. The use of the kye is a practice unique to Filipino Americans.

4. A greater percentage of Asian Indians in the United States have college degrees than does the general population.

5. Given the improved diplomatic relations between the United States and Vietnam, many Vietnamese Americans wish to relocate permanently to Vietnam.

6. Slavery was a significant component of the economic structure of colonial Hawaii.

7. According to the text, Hawaii's race relations are characterized more by compatibility than conflict.

8. The high school dropout rate for Asian Americans is increasing rapidly.

9. With the increasing economic success of Asian Americans, levels of anti-Asian American violence have decreased.

10. Elements of Chinese culture foster the political involvement of Chinese Americans.

Completion
Write in the word or words that best completes the following statements:

1. Korean-American immigrants who accompanied their parents to the United States when young have been termed the _____, or "1.5 generation."

2. A special form of development capital used by Korean Americans to subsidize businesses is called a _____.

3. The Filipino immigrants arriving in the early twentieth century in Hawaii to work on sugar plantations came during the _____ of four distinct periods of Filipino immigration.

4. Despite their long history of immigration to the United States, _____ Americans have not developed visible commercial centers.

5. Stereotyping Asian immigrants in the worst possible light is known as the

_____.

6. The term frequently used to refer to Whites in Hawaii is _____.

7. A clear indication of the multicultural nature of Hawaii is the degree to which members of different racial or ethnic groups marry outside their own group. This is known as _____.

8. The _____ _____ _____ , also known as the Hawaiian Nation, is seeking to have Hawaiian native people receive federal recognition similar to that accorded to mainland tribes.

9. Asian Americans have become _____ in the economy, doing well in small businesses but rarely holding top executive positions.

10. _____ _____ refers to the generalized prejudice toward Asian people and their customs.

Essay Questions

Answer the following questions to the best of your ability. Be sure to support your answers thoroughly.

1. As in previous chapters, the concept of panethnicity is discussed here as possible means for gaining equality in the United States. In your opinion, is it possible for members of the Asian American community to develop a panethnic identity? If so, how? If not, why not? What would be the benefits (economic, political, social) of developing such an identity? What would be the disadvantages? Explain your answer and support your assertions using concepts and other material from your text.

2. Explain the practice of the kye used in the development of capital among Korean Americans. Would such a practice work within other racial or ethnic groups in the United States? If so, within which groups and why? Why should such a practice not work within some racial or ethnic groups? Explain your answer, using material from this chapter and information gained in your reading of previous chapters.

3. Tourism in Hawaii is greatly promoted on the mainland, often along with a picture of its harmonious ethnic and racial diversity that greatly differs from the images we receive of other areas in the United States. Considering what you have just read of the reality of racial and ethnic pluralism in Hawaii, discuss whether or not this picture is entirely accurate. What function does the perpetuation of Hawaii as a culturally pluralist haven serve? What inequalities may be hidden by such an image? Be certain to explain your answer and support your assertions.

CHAPTER 12

Chinese Americans and Japanese Americans

I. LEARNING OBJECTIVES

1. To understand the similarities and differences between the experiences of Japanese Americans and Chinese Americans.
2. To learn about the migration of Chinese and Japanese people to the United States.
3. To learn about prejudice and discrimination affecting Chinese and Japanese Americans, including the evacuation of Japanese Americans during World War II.
4. To understand the economic situation of Japanese and Chinese Americans.
5. To learn about the current status of Chinatowns in the United States.
6. To learn about the roles of family and religion among Japanese and Chinese Americans.

II. CHAPTER OVERVIEW

While many Americans tend to see Asian Americans as one group, the experiences of Japanese Americans and Chinese Americans illustrate the differences between these groups. Japanese Americans experienced extreme discrimination during World War II, but have since managed to maintain a level of economic success. Chinese Americans, who have a longer history in the United States, adapted to their new country by establishing Chinatowns which continue to give this community many strengths and weaknesses. In this chapter, Schaefer also compares and contrasts these two groups in the areas of family and religion, and in the continuing ramifications of prejudice and discrimination.

A. Chinese Americans. Before the great European migrations to the U.S. began in the 1880s, there were already 100,000 Chinese living here. This section explores the history and economic situation of Chinese Americans and Chinatowns, as well as Chinese American family life.
1. How were Chinese perceived by people in the western United States during the 1800s?
2. What has been the pattern of Chinese immigration since 1943?
3. What are the predominant occupations among Chinese Americans?
4. Why have Chinatowns been an important source of employment for Chinese Americans? Why are Chinatowns still important for recent immigrants?
5. What are the tsu, the hui kuan, and the tongs?
6. Why have White Americans not understood the social problems of Chinatown communities?
7. What are the similarities and differences between Chinese American and White American family lives?
8. Why do some Chinese youth turn to gangs?

B. Japanese Americans. This section explores the history of Japanese Americans in the U.S., including the evacuation during World War II. It also discusses the economic situation and the religious and family life of Japanese Americans in the U.S. today.

1. With which terms do Japanese Americans distinguish among generations of immigrants?
2. What incident sparked anti-Japanese American fears during World War II? What was the evidence to back these fears?
3. What were the goals of Executive Order 9066? What were the criteria for confinement? How did most Japanese Americans respond to their confinement?
4. Why were Japanese Americans targeted for evacuation, while German and Italian Americans were ignored?
5. What does the language "relocation centers" and "evacuees" obscure?
6. What was the impact of the camps on the economic situation of Japanese Americans? How have Japanese Americans fared in the last half century?
7. How does the role of religion in Japanese life affect the lives of Japanese Americans?

C. Remnants of Prejudice and Discrimination. This section examines subtle forms of prejudice and discrimination still faced by Chinese and Japanese Americans, and some of the ways that members of these groups attempt to maintain cultural identities.
1. Why might the successes of Japanese Americans actually serve to erode cultural traditions?
2. What does increasing intermarriage reveal about assimilation?
3. How do young Japanese Americans strive to preserve their cultural identity?

III. CRITICAL THINKING QUESTIONS

1. What factors contribute to the different rates of assimilation for Japanese Americans and Chinese Americans? Do you think this pattern will change over time? Why, or why not? Use specific examples to illustrate your answer.

2. According to the text, why have Japanese Americans been more successful than other minorities in the United States? What do you think are the most significant reasons behind their success? Explain why these factors may not be available for other groups.

IV. KEY TERMS

Listed below are some of the key terms introduced in Chapter 12. After having read the chapter and completed the overview on the previous pages, check your comprehension of these terms by writing down the definitions in the space provided in your own words. You can review your work by directing your attention to the Key Terms section at the end of your text.

evacuees
hui kuan
Issei
Kibei
Nisei
Sansei
tongs
tsu
Yonsei

V. TEST QUESTIONS

Multiple Choice Questions
Choose the correct answer from the choices provided.

1. Why was Chinese immigration to the U.S. both welcome and unwelcome at the same time?
a. Americans thought the Chinese were friendly but had strange traditions.
b. They provided hard-working labor, but came with an alien culture.
c. Americans liked Chinese food, but feared Yellow Peril.
d. Americans liked Chinese traditions but didn't really understand them.

2. Which of these was NOT an accusation leveled at Japanese Americans after the bombing of Pearl Harbor?
a. They were accused of helping Japan with the attack.
b. They were accused of poisoning drinking water.
c. They were accused of blocking traffic to the harbor.
d. They were accused of training kamikazes on American land.

3. Japanese American behavior in the concentration camps during World War II:
a. was marked by rebellion and hostility.
b. reaffirmed their loyalty to the United States.
c. showed loss of hope that they would ever be allowed to go free.
d. was marked by many cases of suicide.

4. The main reason Japanese Americans were treated so despicably during World War II was:
a. their lack of resistance.
b. acts of sabotage were widespread.
c. many were operating as spies.
d. racism.

5. In 1940, _____ percent of Japanese Americans lived on the West coast, which dropped to _____ percent by 1950.
a. 89; 58
b. 96; 63
c. 75; 25
d. 50; 40

6. If it weren't for _____, many new Chinese immigrants would remain isolated and unemployed.
a. affirmative action.
b. English as a Second Language courses.
c. Chinatowns.
d. professional skills.

7. The Chinese associations known as _____ are rooted in the Chinese history of unity between families with common ancestry.

a. hui kuan

b. tongs

c. tsu

d. tao

8. The problems in Chinatowns include:

a. dilapidated housing.

b. sweatshop labor.

c. rising crime rates.

d. all of the above.

9. One example of the legacy of China in Chinese American families is:

a. the importance of extended family.

b. lack of parental authority.

c. a high divorce rate.

d. families that only have one child.

10. Nisei Week celebrations are held to:

a. remember the legacy of the Japanese American detention camps.

b. honor Japanese traditions.

c. honor Chinese traditions.

d. reinvigorate Little Tokyos.

True/False Questions

For each of the following statements, determine whether it is true or false. Write your answer in the space provided.

1. The Sansei are first generation immigrants from Japan.

2. The U.S. government had plenty of evidence to support the relocation of Japanese Americans during World War II.

3. Japanese Americans returning home from the World War II camps were warmly received by their White neighbors.

4. At least part of the reason why Japanese Americans were targeted for concentration camps while German and Italian Americans were ignored was that many of those making the decisions were of German and Italian ancestry.

5. Japanese Americans are seen as successful by both occupational and academic standards.

6. Chinese Americans tend to be underrepresented in managerial and professional positions.

7. One function of the Chinese hui kuan associations is to help new immigrants adjust to a new life.

8. Chinatown communities grow more homogenous as time passes.

9. Middle-class White Americans tend to find Japanese American family values strange and hard to accept.

10. Sansei are more active in political protests than Nisei.

Completion
Write in the word or words that best completes the following statements:

1. The _____ _____ _____ of 1913 prohibited those ineligible for citizenship from holding land and limited leases to three years.

2. Japanese Americans forced to resettle in camps during World War II were known as _____.

3. After hearing the case _____ _____ v. _____ _____, the Supreme Court ruled that the detainment of Japanese Americans was unconstitutional.

4. Reagan signed the _____ _____ _____ in 1988 which authorized the payment of $20,000 tax-free to survivors of the Japanese American camps of World War II.

5. Henry Han Xi Lau tells us his Kung Fu Crew works hard like the nerds but identifies with the _____.

6. New immigration has increased Chinatown's dependence on _____.

7. Chinese secret societies known as _____ are based on members' interests rather than locale or family.

8. _____ _____ was the first Chinese American mayor of Monterey Park, California.

9. In Japan, one can be a Shinto and a _____ at the same time.

10. The higher rate of _____ indicates that Whites have become more accepting of Chinese Americans.

Essay Questions

Answer the following questions to the best of your ability. Be sure to support your answers thoroughly.

1. As explained in the text, the immigration patterns of Chinese Americans and Japanese Americans have been different over time. What are some of these differences? How do you think they shaped the experiences of these two groups in the United States? Are there other factors that you think are more important in creating such differences? Why or why not? Be sure to explain your answer thoroughly with specific examples.

2. Chapter 12 offers a detailed discussion of the causes and effects of the Japanese detention camps during World War II. What are the reasons given as to why the camps were instituted? Which of these do you think offers the best explanation of the camps' existence? Explain why you think some reasons are more significant than others. How would a conflict theorist and a functionalist explain the use of the camps? What does this period in history illustrate about the United States and minorities?

3. Chinatowns are an important source of cultural identity for many Chinese Americans although they are not without their problems. Historically, what have been the strengths and benefits of Chinatowns for Chinese Americans? Are these needs now obsolete? What are some of the problems facing Chinatowns and how might they be addressed? Do you think Chinatowns should be allowed to phase out and that Chinese Americans should become more assimilated? Carefully defend your answer addressing the complexities of the issues mentioned in the text.

CHAPTER 13

Jewish Americans: Quest to Maintain Identity

I. LEARNING OBJECTIVES

1. To explore the definition of Jewish identity and to understand the importance of this for Jewish people both inside and outside the United States.
2. To gain an understanding of the migration patterns of Jewish people to the United States and how this has influenced the formation of a Jewish identity.
3. To learn of the origins and impacts of anti-Semitism on the lives and culture of Jewish people.
4. To gain an understanding of the present situation of Jewish people in the United States with regard to their employment, education, and organizational and political activity.
5. To explore the importance of family, religion and cultural heritage to Jewish identity and Jewish culture in the United States.

II. CHAPTER OVERVIEW

As with other racial and ethnic groups, maintaining group solidarity and thus group identity for Jewish people in the United States can be essential to surviving their subordinate status. Paradoxically, the reduction in anti-Semitism present in the United States also poses a threat to the Jewishness or Yiddishkait of Jewish people. This chapter explores the definition of Jewish identity and the origins and impacts of anti-Semitism on the formation of this identity. In addition, the current situation of Jewish people in the United States with regard to employment, education, and organizational and political activity is explored. This chapter also examines the importance of family, religion, and cultural heritage to Jewish identity while addressing the struggles Jewish women face in the double jeopardy they experience in being both female and Jewish.

A. The Jewish People: Race or Religion or Ethnic Group? This section attempts to answer the difficult and lingering question of what is a Jewish person. Elements of race, religion, and ethnicity are considered.
1. How do Jews fulfill the characteristics of a subordinate group? Why is it inaccurate to speak of a "Jewish race?"
2. What is Judaization? How has this affected the assimilation of Jewish people in the United States?

B. Migration of Jews to the United States. This section examines the migration patterns of Jewish people to the United States and how they have influenced the development of a Jewish identity.
1. Why were Jewish immigrants in the United States in the early part of the twentieth century more likely to stay in the United States than other European immigrants? What was the role of anti-Semitism in this process?
2. Why did Jewish refugees who emigrated from Poland, Hungary, and the Ukraine tend to be religiously orthodox and adapt slowly to the ways of the earlier Jewish immigrants?

C. Anti-Semitism Past and Present. This section discusses the origins of anti-Semitism and the ways in which Jewish people have struggled to overcome this hatred. It also explores the history of anti-Semitism in the United States.

1. As the text indicates, the stereotype that Jewish people are obsessed with money is false. How did such a stereotype originate? How does this relate to the fringe-of-values theory?

2. How does the stereotype of Jewish people being clannish relate to Merton's notion that in-group virtues become out-group vices? How does this stereotype fail to consider the extent to which Jewish people have experienced anti-Semitism?

3. How has the fact that anti-Semitism has never been institutionalized in the United States influenced the lives of Jewish Americans?

4. How has the rise in anti-Semitic incidents called attention to this issue? In your opinion, how has this rise affected the identities and culture of Jewish Americans?

5. How did the Zionism resolution affect the lives of Jewish people and their fears about the rise of anti-Semitism?

D. Position of Jewish Americans. This section provides an overview of the present situation of Jewish people in the United States with regard to employment, education, and organizational and political activity.

1. What threat does the secularization of Jewish children pose to Jewish identity? What can be done to reduce this threat?

2. Why would the United States Supreme Court rule that private social organizations may discriminate against Jews and any other racial or ethnic group? What has been the impact of this on Jewish organizations?

E. Religious Life. This section explores the importance of religion to the culture and identity of Jewish people in the United States.

1. If religion is generally unimportant to the majority of Jewish people in the United States, why do the majority of Jewish people belong to synagogues? What is the role of religious tradition in maintaining Jewish identity?

F. Jewish Identity. This section explores the factors that influence the identity and group solidarity of Jewish people in the United States.

1. What are the positive and negative effects of racial and ethnic identification?

2. How has the diminishing of hostility directed at Jewish people shaped Jewish identity? Is it possible for Jews to shed their identity entirely? Why or why not?

3. What are the unique identity issues that present themselves to Jewish women? How is this double jeopardy similar to that experienced by women of other ethnic and racial groups discussed earlier in the text?

4. What are the problems that the Jewish family faces in its role in identity transmission?
How are these problems similar to those faced by members of other religious or ethnic groups?

5. How are the changes in Jewish identity similar to the changes experienced by third and fourth-generation members of other racial or ethnic groups?

III. CRITICAL THINKING QUESTIONS

1. What is peoplehood? What are the factors that lead to a sense of peoplehood for those who belong to the Jewish ethnic group? In your own life, do you have a sense of peoplehood? If so, what factors contribute to this? If not, what do you think prevents you from developing a sense of peoplehood? Explain your answer.

2. As your text indicates, anti-Semitism has been displayed by some African Americans. What do you see as the reason for an oppressed group participating in the oppression of others? In your discussion use examples other than the conflict between Jews and African Americans. For example, consider the conflict between Korean Americans and African Americans, between White ethnic immigrants and Asian immigrants, and so on.

IV. KEY TERMS

Listed below are some of the key terms introduced in Chapter 13. After having read the chapter and completed the overview on the previous pages, check your comprehension of these terms by writing down the definitions in the space provided in your own words. You can review your work by directing your attention to the Key Terms section at the end of your text.

anti-Semitism
fringe-of-values theory
halakha
Holocaust
Holocaust revisionists
in-group virtues
Judaization
kashrut
marginality
out-group vices
peoplehood
Yiddishkait
Zionism

V. TEST QUESTIONS

Multiple Choice Questions
Choose the correct answer from the choices provided.

1. The largest population of Jewish people in the world reside in:
a. Israel.
b. Russia.
c. Argentina.
d. the United States.

2. Within the United States, the majority of the Jewish population resides in:
a. the Midwest.
b. the South.
c. the Northeast.
d. the West.

3. The primary component of Jewish identity is:
a. religion.
b. ethnicity.
c. race.
d. political beliefs.

4. Jewish people originally from Spain and Portugal are said to be of what origin?
a. Eastern European
b. Orthodox
c. Sephardic
d. Western European

5. Jews are more likely than the general population to label themselves:
a. conservative
b. liberal
c. apolitical
d. independent

6. In the 1920s and 1930s, anti-Semites in the United States like Henry Ford linked Jewish people with:
a. the Great Depression.
b. the decrease in church attendance.
c. Communism.
d. a decline in values.

7. There is a Jewish-founded university in commemoration of which of the following people?
a. Leland Stanford Jr.
b. Moses Brown
c. Louis Brandeis
d. John Harvard

8. Which of the following is NOT a sect of Judaism in the United States?
a. Liberal
b. Reform
c. Conservative
d. Orthodox

9. Which of the following sects of Judaism has altered many Jewish rituals and supported outreach programs to convert people to Judaism?
a. Conservative
b. Reform
c. Orthodox
d. Hasidim

10. The Jewish law covering obligations and duties is known as:
a. halakha.
b. kosher.
c. kashrut.
d. Talmud.

True/False Questions

For each of the following statements, determine whether it is true or false. Write your answer in the space provided.

1. Jewish cultural heritage is nationalistic in origin.

2. Most of the Jewish immigrants who migrated to the United States up to the early twentieth century came voluntarily.

3. Jewish immigrants to the United States when compared to other Europeans are more likely to return to their home country.

4. According to the text, many Gentiles today believe Jewish people use underhanded methods in business and finance.

5. For Jewish people, the desire for formal schooling stems from their religion.

6. The United Jewish Appeal (UJA) represents all American Jews.

7. The United States Supreme Court has consistently ruled that private social organizations may discriminate against Jews.

8. The majority of Jews in Israel are religiously observant.

9. Orthodox Jews represent the poorest sect of Judaism.

10. Jewish people in the United States today are just as likely to marry a Gentile as a Jew.

Completion
Write in the word or words that best completes the following statements:

1. Anti-Jewish prejudice and discrimination is referred to as _____ _____.

2. The lessening of the importance of Judaism as a religion and the substitution of cultural tradition as the tie that binds Jews is called _____.

3. Gordon Allport asserts that the perpetuation of Anti-Semitism is related to Christians incorrectly believing Jews to be involved in business practices that were on the edge of the realm of proper conduct. His theory is known as the _____ _____ _____.

4. Sociologist Robert Merton described how proper behavior by one's own group becomes unacceptable when practiced by outsiders by stating that in-group virtues become _____ _____ _____.

5. The _____ _____ of B'nai B'rith, was founded to monitor and fight against anti-Semitism and hate crimes direct at other groups.

6. _____, initially referring to Jewish religious yearning to return to the biblical homeland, has been expressed in the twentieth century in the movement to create a Jewish state in Palestine.

7. The _____ _____ _____ was founded in 1939 and serves as a fund-raising organization for humanitarian causes.

8. According to Marshall Sklare, "The thrust of Jewish religious culture is _____ [while] the thrust of the American religious culture is moralistic."

9. The Jewish laws pertaining to permissible and forbidden foods is referred to as the _____.

10. Another term for Jewish identity or "Jewishness" is _____.

Essay Questions
Answer the following questions to the best of your ability. Be sure to support your answers thoroughly.

1. As with many subordinate groups, what may be acceptable for the dominant group to do may be unacceptable for the subordinate group to do. Merton referred to this as in-group virtues becoming out-group vices. What examples do you see of this phenomenon in our stereotypes about people who are Jewish? Using the conflict perspective, analyze why this phenomenon occurs and discuss its

impact on the lives of Jews and non-Jews. In your answer, be certain to incorporate concepts from the text to strengthen your answer.

2. The text mentions on several occasions that Jewish identity is threatened by the secularization of Jewish children. How is the threat to Jewish identity similar to that experienced by other immigrant groups through the process of assimilation? Using Hansen's principle of third generation interest (discussed in Chapter 5), discuss whether you think that there will be a resurgence in Jewish identity. Do you think such a resurgence is necessary? How will it help or hinder the position of Jewish people in the social hierarchy in the United States? Explain your answer and support your assertions thoroughly.

3. The text mentions briefly the unique identity issue faced by Jewish women, whose religious tradition has placed them in a subordinate position. Is it possible for Jewish women to challenge their subordinate position and yet still maintain their Jewish identity? What impact will such a challenge have on the group identity of Jewish people? What similarities can you draw between the experiences of Jewish women and women of other subordinate racial or ethnic groups? Explain your answer and support your assertions using concepts and other materials from the text.

CHAPTER 14

Women: The Oppressed Majority

I. LEARNING OBJECTIVES

1. To learn why women are defined as a subordinate group.
2. To understand the impact of gender roles in perpetuating inequalities between women and men.
3. To learn how conflict theory, functionalism, and labeling theory explain gender role socialization.
4. To explore the history and contemporary concerns of the feminist movement.
5. To understand how women are treated differently than men in the economy, in education, in the family, and in politics.
6. To learn about "double jeopardy" and what this means for minority women.

II. CHAPTER OVERVIEW

As the chapter title suggests, women are a numerical majority in the population but they fulfill the properties of a subordinate group. In this chapter, Schaefer examines the different sociological explanations as to why the subordination of women persists, and how their situation is comparable to that of racial minorities in the United States. He also introduces the history of the women's movement, and the barriers to equality in aspects of social life such as the economy, education, family, and politics. Finally, we see how minority women are faced with unique challenges.

1. What are some parallel stereotypes that illustrate similarities between how women and Blacks have been viewed by society?

2. What is sexism? What alternative view of the sexes does the concept of androgyny offer?

A. Gender Roles. From birth, girls and boys are socialized to behave differently. This section explains gender roles and how they shape interactions between women and men.
1. What are gender roles? List some examples not given in the text of traits we tend to see as masculine and traits we define as feminine.
2. What do the findings of sociologists Miller and Adler illustrate about the gender role socialization of children?
3. What are some examples of the evidence that gender roles are socially constructed?

B. Sociological Perspectives. Gender differentiation is an integral part of the lifelong process of socialization. Functionalism, conflict theory, and labeling theory all explain the persistence of gender socialization in different ways.
1. What is the functionalist view of sex differentiation? What are the weaknesses of this perspective?
2. How would a conflict theorist characterize the relationship between females and males in our society? Why would a conflict theorist advocate change in the social structures in this case?
3. What is the emphasis of the labeling perspective in explaining the continuation of gender roles?

C. The Feminist Movement. The women's movement for equality, like similar movements for other groups, has been marked by many struggles in the United States, including both the suffrage movement and the women's liberation movement.
1. Who were the suffragists? When did they accomplish their goal?
2. Why might focusing on the vote for women have been detrimental to feminism as a whole?
3. What social events inhibited success for the women's movement in the mid-1960s?
4. What was the Equal Rights Amendment and what led to its defeat?
5. Why is male liberation a logical counterpart to female liberation?
6. Why was the concept of the feminine mystique important during the women's movement of the 1960s? How has this focus shifted over time?

D. The Economic Picture. Comparing women's and men's occupational attainments illustrates the continued economic subordination of women. Sex discrimination is institutionalized in the work force, while issues such as sexual harassment and the feminization of poverty further highlight women's economic oppression.
1. What are some examples of sex segregation in occupations, as illustrated by Table 14.1? How can you relate these divisions to gender role socialization?
2. Why is there a lag between laws and reality in the area of sex discrimination?
3. Why doesn't the Equal Pay Act of 1963 help many women to earn salaries comparable to men?
4. What is pay equity? Why is it difficult to enforce?
5. What is the glass ceiling, and what factors contribute to keeping it in place?
6. How does the concept of the mommy track exacerbate women's challenges in the workplace?
7. What is sexual harassment? How would a conflict theorist explain this phenomenon?
8. What is the feminization of poverty? Why are displaced homemakers a part of this developing problem?

E. Education. Although women now have access to higher education, girls and women continue to be treated differently from boys and men at all levels of the educational system.
1. What are some of the ways that girls and boys are treated differently in schools? What outcomes does this treatment encourage?
2. What are the goals of Title IX? Why is it seen as controversial and what does this illustrate about sexism in our society?

F. Family Life. The family is a social institution which highlights the vastly different expectations our society has of women and men, especially in regard to child care and housework.
1. What factors do you think contribute to the lack of involvement of men in child care?
2. How do most women feel about the uneven distribution of housework, according to Lennon and Rosenfield?
3. What is the second shift and what does it illustrate about the effects of gender roles on wives and husbands?
4. Why is abortion seen as connected to family life by both "prochoice" and "prolife" groups?

G. Political Activity. Women remain underrepresented in public office despite the fact that they comprise 53 percent of voters and have a strong history of political involvement.

1. What has been the most serious barrier for women interested in holding public office? What type of treatment are they likely to encounter once elected?

2. What are some examples of women's political activities beyond running for office?

H. Double Jeopardy: Minority Women. Many women face the double oppression of being female and a racial or ethnic minority in a sexist and racist society. This section touches on some of the struggles unique to these women.

1. What is double jeopardy? Why does this put minority women in a difficult position when it comes to anti-sexist and anti-racist movements?

2. What are some ways that the situations of Black women, Native American women, and Chicanas are different from that of White women?

3. What is the debate between Black nationalism and Black feminism?

III. CRITICAL THINKING QUESTIONS

1. As illustrated by Chapter 14, what are some of the many ways that the subordination of women parallels the subordination of racial minorities in this society? Where do the comparisons fall short? Overall, do you think that analogy is a useful one? Why or why not?

2. In your opinion, what is the relationship between institutionalized sexism and the persistence of sexual harassment in the workplace? In addition, do you think such harassment is encouraged by gender role socialization? Explain why you do or do not think these concepts are related, drawing on evidence presented in the text and examples from your own experience.

IV. KEY TERMS

Listed below are some of the key terms introduced in Chapter 14. After having read the chapter and completed the overview on the previous pages, check your comprehension of these terms by writing down the definitions in the space provided in your own words. You can review your work by directing your attention to the Key Terms section at the end of your text.

androgyny
displaced homemakers
double jeopardy
feminine mystique
feminization of poverty
gender roles
glass ceiling
mommy track
pay equity
second shift
sexism
sexual harassment
suffragists

V. TEST QUESTIONS

Multiple Choice Questions
Choose the correct answer from the choices provided.

1. _____ refers to the ideology that one sex is superior to the other, while the view that people's differences are not sex-based is known as _____.
a. Androgyny; sexism
b. Sexism, androgyny
c. Patriarchy, humanism
d. Male dominance, sociobiology

2. Functionalists see sex differentiation as:
a. discriminatory and wrong.
b. perpetuated largely by the media.
c. biologically based.
d. a useful way to divide labor within families.

3. Susan B. Anthony was arrested in 1872 for:
a. trying to vote in that years presidential election.
b. planning to assassinate the president.
c. performing illegal abortions.
d. having women publicly demonstrate for their rights.

4. What factor contributed to the delay of progress for the women's movement in the 1960s?
a. the sexism of the New Left
b. the fact that different groups were focused on different struggles
c. existing women's groups avoided feminism
d. all of the above

5. Which of the following is NOT a major barrier to woman's executive advancement?
a. lack of access to informal networks of communication.
b. less initiative and stamina
c. little access to developmental assignments
d. lack of mentoring

6. According to the findings of one study, African American women are _____ times more likely than White women to experience sexual harassment at work.
1. ten
b. five
c. three
d. two

7. One of the provisions of Title IX is that:
a. schools must end sexist hiring practices.
b. teachers must praise girls as much as boys.
c. girls will be steered towards the sciences, while boys will be encouraged to find a wife to support them.
d. single-sex schools will be banned by 2010.

8. Which of the following is NOT an aspect of women's experience that is shared with racial or ethnic minorities?
a. increasing awareness of subordinate status and group solidarity
b. involuntary membership in a subordinate group
c. low rates of intermarriage with the dominant group
d. unequal treatment relative to the dominant group

9. Out of 435 Congressional representatives in 1999, the number of women elected was:
a. 217
b. 109
c. 59
d. 14

10. Chicanas have traditionally been excluded from decision-making in both the
_____ and the _____.
a. family; workplace
b. cantinas; church
c. government; women's movement
d. family; church

True/False Questions
For each of the following statements, determine whether it is true or false. Write your answer in the space provided.

1. Even young children are aware of the appropriate gender roles.

2. Conflict theorists recognize the unequal distribution of power between men and women.

3. Suffrage for women was a quick and easy accomplishment.

4. The success of the Equal Rights Amendment made the women's movement very popular.

5. The wage gap between women and men is easily explained by differences in education and employment experience.

6. The feminization of poverty refers to the fact that the poor only have access to "women's work" if they have access to work at all.

7. Child care is still overwhelmingly the responsibility of women.

8. The concept of the second shift refers to the fact that women have to do twice the amount of work as men to be considered half as good.

9. The League of Women Voters works to educate the public about political candidates.

10. Arlie Hochschild says that society on the whole has changed since the 1960s but the situation of women has not changed as much.

Completion
Write in the word or words that best completes the following statements:

1. Society's expectations of proper behavior for women and men is known as _____.

2. The _____ _____ focuses on the media and how it continues to portray women and men in traditional roles.

3. The _____ _____ gave women the right to vote.

4. The concept of the _____ _____ refers to women seeing themselves only as wives and mothers.

5. The _____ _____ remains a barrier for women attempting to gain access to high management positions in corporations.

6. _____ _____ are women who worked as wives and mothers while married, but could not find full-time employment after being divorced, separated, or widowed.

7. According to Walzer's findings, mothers even spend more time _____ about child care than fathers do.

8. The Supreme Court decision in _____ v. _____ gave women the right to legal abortion, although not without restrictions.

9. The oppression of minority women is sometimes referred to as _____ _____.

10. According to the text, advocates of Black _____ contend that feminism only distracts women from full participation in the African American struggle.

Essay Questions

Answer the following questions to the best of your ability. Be sure to support your answers thoroughly.

1. How do functionalism, conflict theory and labeling theory explain gender roles? In light of the information presented in Chapter 14, which theory do you think makes the most sense? Choose two areas of social life (the economy, education, family or politics) and how the theory you have chosen would explain the position of women in these areas. In addition explain why you think the other two theories are inadequate. Use specific examples to defend your answer.

2. In the economy, women tend to be paid less than men and are underrepresented in upper level positions. In family life, even women with careers are more involved with childcare and housework than their husbands. Do you think that there is a relationship between women's experiences in the work force and at home? Why or why not? Some theorists believe that the solution to women's inequality lies in equal pay for equal work and in paid housework. Do you agree? Why? What solutions would you suggest? Be sure to be specific as you explain your answer.

3. What role has the issue of sexual harassment played in recent debates about the position of women in the workforce? According to the text, what is the evolving legal definition of sexual harassment? When does flirting become sexual harassment? As the workforce is increasingly made up of both men and women, do you think more or fewer people will develop relationships in the workplace? What does this issue tell us about power in the workplace?

CHAPTER 15

Beyond the United States: The Comparative Perspective

I. LEARNING OBJECTIVES

1. To gain an understanding of how racial and ethnic differences differ from society to society, focusing on Mexico, Canada, Northern Ireland, Israel, and South Africa.
2. To understand the status of women on a global level and how it compares to the status of women in the United States.
3. To gain further understanding of the social construction of race.
4. To increase our understanding of how issues of identity and culture both unify and divide communities and nations.
5. To understand the nature of conflict based on religious differences in Northern Ireland.
6. To examine the foundations of the conflict between Israelis and Palestinians as well as consider the likelihood of resolution of this conflict.
7. To gain an understanding of the impact of colonialism and apartheid on current race relations in South Africa.

II. CHAPTER OVERVIEW

Mexico, Canada, Northern Ireland, Israel, and South Africa have remarkable similarities and differences in their relationships between dominant and subordinate groups. This chapter examines these similarities and differences, noting the impact of factors such as colonialism, race constructs, segregation, assimilation, and gender stratification. In addition, the similarities and differences between these areas of the world and the United States are explored. Finally, this chapter aids in the understanding of the global nature of dominant and subordinate relations along the lines of race, ethnicity, religion, and gender.

A. Mexico. This section discusses the complexity of the nation of Mexico and its issues of inequality. In addition, this section sheds light on the relationship of Mexico and its people to the United States as well as the status of women within Mexico.
1. Why is there a major need in contemporary Mexico to reassess the relations between the indigenous peoples and the government of Mexico? How does this relate to the development of a national culture in Mexico?
2. What was *indigenismo*? How did it affect the lives of indigenous people?
3. What are the different divisions of the color gradient in Mexico? How are these similar to different from racial divisions in the United States? How is this demonstrative of the social construction of race?

4. What is the status of women in Mexico? How does it compare with that of women in the United States? What factors contribute to this difference? What steps are women in Mexico taking to address their subordinate status? What has been the impact of their efforts?

B. Canada. This section dispels the myth of Canada as a homogeneous nation, discussing the efforts to develop a policy of multiculturalism in order to legislate a pluralistic society. In addition, it focuses on the treatment of the Aboriginal Peoples and the Quebecois as well as on the impact of immigration on Canadian multiculturalism.
1. What has been the relationship of Canada with its native people? How is the relationship similar to or different from the relationship between the United States and Native Americans?
2. What have been the efforts of the Quebecois to reassert their identity? What has been the impact on the people of Quebec specifically and on the nation of Canada as a whole?
3. Why did the referendum developed from the Charlottetown agreement fail? How do the language and cultural issues related to it both unify and divide the nation of Canada?
4. How does the image that people in the United States have of race relations in Canada differ from the social reality? What fosters the image of Canada as a land of positive intergroup relations?

C. Northern Ireland. This section discusses the roots of the armed conflict between Protestants and Roman Catholics that continues in Northern Ireland. In addition, it discusses the feasibility of proposed solutions to this conflict.
1. How does the history of colonialism and anti-colonial resistance relate to the current conflict in Northern Ireland?
2. How do social issues such as employment and family structure compound the political problems faced by Roman Catholics in Northern Ireland?
3. Why are the minority Roman Catholics and the majority Protestants reluctant to implement a political compromise in Northern Ireland? Is this situation similar to that of other conflicts in the United States and elsewhere the world? What are the possible solutions to the conflict in Northern Ireland, and how would they affect each group?

D. Israel and the Palestinians. This section discusses the origins of the conflict between Israel, its Arab neighbors, and the Palestinians. In addition, it outlines the issues that remain to be resolved after the signing of the Israeli-Palestinian peace accord.
1. What is the role of the Diaspora and Zionism in the conflict between Jews and Palestinians?
2. According to the sociologist Ernest Krautz, what are the "two nations"? What are the relations between the groups referred to in this term?
3. What was the Intifada? What factors led to this act of resistance? What did its broad range of participants demonstrate? Why is the Intifada significant?

E. Republic of South Africa. This section discusses the impact of colonialism and apartheid on current race relations in South Africa?
1. What were pass laws? What were they intended to do? How were they related to the system of apartheid? What was the system of apartheid intended to do?
2. What are the issues facing the African National Congress in its role as the first post-apartheid government? How do these compare with issues in the United States today?

III. CRITICAL THINKING QUESTIONS

1. What patterns of intergroup relations currently existing today are similar to the policy of apartheid? Provide examples and explain similarities that you see.

2. What legacies of colonialism are common to each of the countries examined in this chapter? How did colonialism pose similar issues in the United States? How are the issues different? Explain your answer.

IV. KEY TERMS

Listed below are some of the key terms introduced in Chapter 15. After having read the chapter and completed the overview on the previous pages, check your comprehension of these terms by writing down the definitions in the space provided in your own words. You can review your work by directing your attention to the Key Terms section at the end of your text.

apartheid
color gradient
Diaspora
ethnonational conflict
home rule
Intifada
pass laws
world systems theory
Zionism

V. TEST QUESTIONS

Multiple Choice Questions
Choose the correct answer from the choices provided.

1. In the Western Hemisphere, Mexico is the _____ largest nation.
a. second
b. fourth
c. third
d. fifth

2. The Mexican government's policy to promote national integration was known as:
a. mestizo
b. indigenismo
c. criollos
d. the color gradient

3. What percentage of Mexican women were in the paid labor force in 1995?
a. 68%
b. 40%
c. 27%
d. 11%

4. Which of the following is NOT a stage of Canadian history?
a. Spanish colonialism
b. French colonialism
c. British colonialism
d. Canadian colonialism

5. Which of the following is NOT a factor of difference between. Protestants and Catholics in Northern Ireland?
a. education
b. income
c. language
d. housing

6. The United Kingdom employs what percentage of the people of Northern Ireland in government jobs?
a. 10%
b. 20%
c. 30%
d. 40%

7. The yearning to establish as Jewish state in the biblical homeland is known as:
a. Zionism.
b. Diaspora.
c. Intifada.
d. Home rule.

8. The uprising in Israel by the Palestinians in the occupies territories known as the:
a. Six-Day War.
b. Ramadan War.
c. Intifada.
d. Yom Kippur War.

9. In 1997, Whites made up _____ percent of the South African population.
a. 2
b. 12.
c. 26
d. 48

10. Which of the following is a controversial issue currently being faced by the post-apartheid government of South Africa?
a. rights of Whites
b. illegal immigration
c. affirmative action
d. all of the above

True/False Questions

For each of the following statements, determine whether it is true or false. Write your answer in the space provided.

1. The existence of many Indian cultures has been seen in this century as an obstacle to the development of a national culture in Mexico.

2. The amendment passed in Mexico in 1992 that protected the languages, cultures, customs, and resources of indigenous Mexican Indian peoples has had a significant impact on the Mexican Indian communities.

3. The *M--etis* along with the Inuit have historically enjoyed separate legal recognition in Canada.

4. After much struggle, a House of Commons seat has been designated for Toronto's Aboriginal Peoples.

5. The failure of the Charlottetown agreement has essentially closed constitutional debate on the recognition of Quebec as a distinct society.

6. The British government has denied Northern Ireland's demands for home rule.

7. The Jewish people residing in Israel are a homogenous group of similar origins and status.

8. The creation of the Palestinian Authority has exacerbated the economic problems of the Palestinians.

9. Apartheid was a system of de facto but not de jure discrimination.

10. Two thirds of the South African population currently lives in homes without electricity or running water.

Completion

Write in the word or words that best completes the following statements:

1. Conflicts between ethnic, racial, religious and linguistic groups within nations are referred to as _____ conflicts.

2. Mexicans intermarrying with Europeans formed a _____ class of people of mixed ancestry.

3. The placement of people on a continuum from light to dark skin color rather than distinct racial groupings is known as a _____ _____.

4. Canadians of mixed racial ancestry (which includes native ancestry) are known as the _____.

5. The granting of a local parliament to Ireland is known as _____ _____.

6. A proposed solution to the hostilities in Northern Ireland to maintain all ties to the United Kingdom would restore dominance by the _____.

7. The exile of Jews from Palestine is known as the _____.

8. The new Jewish population of Israel grew under the country's _____ _____ _____.

9. A policy of separate development, created by Whites in South Africa to ensure their dominance, was known as _____.

10. South Africa's first democratically elected president was _____ _____.

Essay Questions
Answer the following questions to the best of your ability. Be sure to support your answers thoroughly.

1. How is the color gradient (mentioned in this chapter as well as Chapters 9 and 10) an example of the social construction of race? If, as the color gradient implies, race can be socially constructed, what would need to take place in order to reconstruct race in a manner that does not continue a pattern of dominant and subordinate intergroup relations? What would prevent such a reconstruction? How would the conflict perspective view the likelihood of such a reconstruction?

2. What is ethnonational conflict? How does world systems theory explain the existence and similarity of conflicts like these in many different countries? What is the role of colonialism in creating the conditions for ethnonational conflicts? Are ethnonational conflicts the outcome of biological differences, ancient tribal allegiances, or recent world political and economic history? Justify your answer with reference to the text.

3. Using both the functionalist and the conflict perspectives, examine the role of indigenous people in places like Canada, Mexico, and the United States in reducing the inequality that they experience. What would each perspective see as a means for improving their subordinate status? Finally, indicate

which perspective you think offers the best explanations and solutions. Be certain to justify your answer and support your assertions.

CHAPTER 16

Overcoming Exclusion

I. LEARNING OBJECTIVES

1. To understand the parallels between the subordinate status of racial minorities and that of the elderly, people with disabilities, and lesbians and gay men.
2. To learn who makes up the elderly population and the issues that concern them the most.
3. To become familiar with the recent gains made by people with physical disabilities.
4. To learn about the barriers facing lesbians and gay men in their struggle for equality.

II. CHAPTER OVERVIEW

While the focus of the text thus far has been on the social disadvantages people experience based on race, ethnicity, religion and gender, unequal treatment extends to other categories of people as well. In this chapter, Schaefer explains how ageism, ableism, and homophobia limit the life chances of many people in the United States. As with racial inequality, improvements have been made, but we cannot ignore the subordination that continues to exist.
1. Compare the analogies of the melting pot, the salad bowl and the kaleidoscope. Which do you think best describes the current situation in the United States?

A. The Aged: A Social Minority. Although a growing proportion of the population is elderly, they still experience prejudice and discrimination. This section examines the challenges facing the elderly and how advocacy groups are addressing these issues.
1. What proportion of the population is elderly? What is the gender, racial, and geographical composition of the elderly population?
2. What is ageism? What are some examples of ageism in our society?
3. What is happening to the poverty rate of the elderly? What are some explanations for this?
4. List three organizations advocating on behalf of the elderly. What are their goals? Why do racial minorities tend to be underrepresented in these groups?

B. People with Disabilities. As with other physical attributes such as race and sex, we make assumptions and treat people differently based on physical ability. People with disabilities won a significant victory with the passage of the Americans with Disabilities Act, but continue to face prejudice and discrimination in many areas of life.
1. What is a disability? What proportion of the population is affected by some type of disability? How do different racial groups experience disability?
2. How does the media tend to portray people with disabilities? How does this relate to Goffman's concept of stigma?
3. What are some examples of individual and institutional discrimination faced by people with disabilities?
4. What are some of the goals of the disability rights movement?

5. In what ways is the passage of the Americans with Disabilities Act a significant success for people with disabilities?

C. Gays and Lesbians: Coming Out for Equality. Like the elderly and people with disabilities, lesbians and gay men have been stigmatized and treated with prejudice and discrimination in the United States. Although the movement for gay and lesbian rights has become more visible and organized in recent years, many institutional barriers to equality persist.
1. What were the findings of the Kinsey reports? How did they challenge common perceptions about sexual behavior?
2. What is homophobia? What are some examples of its presence in different areas of social life?
3. How do the initial response to the AIDS crisis and the Supreme Court decision in *Bowers v. Hardwick* illustrate institutionalized homophobia?
4. What are domestic partnership benefits? Why is this an important issue for many lesbians and gay men?

D. The Glass Half Empty. There is no doubt that oppressed groups in the United States have made gains in many ways over the years. However, such successes should not remove our focus from the vast inequalities that still exist.
1. What are some examples of how the situation of African Americans and Hispanics has improved over time? How does our perception of these improvements change if we compare their current situation to that of Whites?

III. CRITICAL THINKING QUESTIONS

1. Of the three analogies of how people interact (melting pot, salad bowl, and kaleidoscope), which do you think best describes the current status of the United States? Which do you think would be best as a goal for this country? Is there another analogy which you find more appropriate? Explain your answer with specific examples.

2. How are the effects of stigma similar for the elderly, people with disabilities, and lesbians and gay men? How are they different? How do you think each group could best address these stigmas? Is this different from how they have been addressed by advocacy groups? Why or why not? Be sure to defend your assertions carefully.

IV. KEY TERMS

Listed below are some of the key terms introduced in Chapter 16. After having read the chapter and completed the overview on the previous pages, check your comprehension of these terms by writing down the definitions in the space provided in your own words. You can review your work by directing your attention to the Key Terms section at the end of your text.

ageism
disability
domestic partnership
homophobia

V. TEST QUESTIONS

Multiple Choice Questions
Choose the correct answer from the choices provided.

1. An analogy of how people in the United States interact that illustrates diversity and dramatic change is the:
a. melting pot.
b. salad bowl.
c. kaleidoscope.
d. internet.

2. Prejudice and discrimination against the elderly is known as:
a. geezerism.
b. ageism.
c. retireeism.
d. osteoporosis.

3. According to the text, the poverty rate among the elderly has _____ in recent years.
a. increased
b. declined
c. remained constant
d. doubled

4. The Gray Panthers work to:
a. combat prejudice and discrimination against the elderly.
b. save endangered species.
c. ensure rights for people with disabilities.
d. win equal rights for gay men and lesbians.

5. If someone has a reduced ability to perform tasks one would normally do at a given stage in life, we consider them to have:
a. a lack of motivation to try harder.
b. a need for daily personal assistance.
c. a disability.
d. very special needs.

6. Mass media contribute to the stereotyping of people with disabilities by:
a. showing the disabled as helpless and childlike.
b. portraying disability as a punishment for evil.
c. focusing on inspirational stories rather than daily realities.
d. all of the above.

7. In order for people with disabilities to continue to win political victories, they should:
a. form a strong political bloc.
b. fight for entitlement privileges.
c. focus on the local level of politics.
d. address companies' employment practices.

8. In a 1992 national survey of sexual behavior, _____ percent of men identified themselves as gay, and _____ of women identified themselves as lesbian.
a. 1.5; 2.8
b. 2.8; 1.5
c. 10; 5.6
d. 28; 15

9. An outspoken and confrontational AIDS activist group which was instrumental in raising public awareness of the AIDS crisis is:
a. PFLAG.
b. SAGE.
c. ACT-UP
d. all of the above.

10. Domestic partnership benefits would:
a. be advantageous for more cohabiting heterosexual couples than gay couples.
b. legitimize the relationships of lesbians and gay men.
c. apply to inheritance, taxation, parenting, health care, housing, and other areas.
d. all of the above.

True/False Questions
For each of the following statements, determine whether it is true or false. Write your answer in the space provided.

1. By 1997, 12.7 percent of the population were sixty-five and over.

2. Research shows that older employees are often an asset to their employers.

3. In 1998, Norman Matloff found no age discrimination in the computer software industry, because it is an understaffed field.

4. Older people of color are emerging as a political force distinct from the elderly population as a whole.

5. Racial minorities experience disabilities at the same rate as Whites.

6. Accessibility in public places is no longer a problem for people with disabilities.

7. Like countries such as Great Britain, the United States sees disability as an entitlement issue.

8. Studies consistently reveal that ten percent of the population consider themselves lesbians, gay men or bisexual.

9.There are more self-identifying homosexuals in rural areas than in cities.

10. The uprising at the Stonewall Inn is seen as the beginning of the contemporary lesbian and gay movement.

Completion
Write in the word or words that best completes the following statements:

1. In comparison with the rest of the population, the elderly are more likely to live in certain states and be _____ and _____.

2. Although age discrimination in employment is illegal, only about _____ percent of law suits alleging such discrimination are won.

3. The _____ _____ _____ _____, an advocacy group for the elderly, represents one out of every four voters in the United States.

4. About _____ million people in the United States have some type of disability.

5. According to labeling theorists, society attaches a _____ to people with disabilities which often leads to discrimination.

6. The _____ _____ _____ Act, which passed in 1990, is the most significant antidiscrimination legislation since the Civil Rights Act of 1964.

7. The research findings of _____ _____ were shocking to the public because they showed homosexual behavior to be more common than previously believed.

8. _____ is the fear of and prejudice towards homosexuality.

9. The Supreme Court decision in _____ v. _____ highlighted the lack of legal rights for gay citizens.

10. Data show that although the situations of many oppressed groups has improved over time, there exists a large _____ between their quality of life and that of the majority.

Essay Questions

Answer the following questions to the best of your ability. Be sure to support your answers thoroughly.

1. In what ways do the experiences of the elderly reflect other inequalities in our society? Are there also ways in which the elderly are unaffected by other forms of oppression? Why or why not? In your answer, consider issues of economic oppression. In what ways do you think the elderly can best address their current situation? Explain your answer and support your assertions.

2. How has the treatment of people with disabilities improved in recent years? What are some significant problems that remain? In your opinion, why have some issues been adequately addressed while others are ignored? What does this illustrate about how our society views disability? Do you think this will continue to change over time? Why or why not? Defend your answer with specific examples.

3. How do the passing of the Defense of Marriage Act and the "Don't Ask, Don't Tell" policy of the United States military show that as lesbians and gay men become more politically active for equal rights, homophobia becomes more institutionalized? What other examples can you think of that illustrate this phenomenon? Has this happened to other groups who have fought for equality? Why or why not? How should advocacy groups for lesbian and gay rights address such institutionalized homophobia? Explain each part of your answer carefully with examples.

ANSWER KEY

Chapter 1 – *Understanding Race and Ethnicity*

Multiple Choice

1. c	2. d	3. b	4. a	5. c
6. c	7. b	8. d	9. b	10. a

True/False

1. F	2. T	3. T	4. F	5. F
6. T	7. T	8. F	9. T	10. F

Completion

1.	minority group	6.	labeling theory
2.	Ethnic groups	7.	self-fulfilling prophecy
3.	racial formation	8.	emigration; immigration
4.	stratification	9.	fusion
5.	functionalist perspective; dysfunctions	10.	marginality

Chapter 2 – *Prejudice*

Multiple Choice

1. b	2. c	3. a	4. b	5. d
6. c	7. d	8. a	9. b	10. d

True/False

1. F	2. T	3. T	4. F	5. T
6. F	7. F	8. T	9. F	10. T

Completion

1.	Ethnophaulisms	6.	ethnic, religious
2.	four	7.	passively
3.	scapegoat	8.	voting
4.	social distance	9.	Mass media, education
5.	Prejudice	10.	equal status contact, common goal

Chapter 3 – *Discrimination*

Multiple Choice

1. c	2. b	3. a	4. c	5. d
6. d	7. d	8. b	9. a	10. d

| 1. T | 2. F | 3. T | 4. F | 5. T |
| 6. F | 7. F | 8. T | 9. T | 10. F |

Completion

1.	double jeopardy	6.	institutional racism
2.	informal economy	7.	states' rights
3.	race	8.	*Martin v. Wilks*
4.	total discrimination	9.	Civil Rights
5.	voluntary associations; federal government	10.	quotas

Chapter 4 – *Immigration and the United States*

Multiple Choice

| 1. c | 2. b | 3. d | 4. c | 5. a |
| 6. c | 7. b | 8. b | 9. a | 10. c |

True/False

| 1. F | 2. T | 3. F | 4. F | 5. T |
| 6. F | 7. F | 8. T | 9. F | 10. F |

Completion

1.	Samuel Morse; Ralph Waldo Emerson	6.	ethnic; racial
2.	sinophobes	7.	Refugees
3.	Asians; Latin Americans	8.	Know-Nothings
4.	illegal aliens	9.	Samuel Gompers
5.	2.35 billion; 2.4 billion	10.	54

Chapter 5 – *Ethnicity and Religion*

Multiple Choice

| 1. c | 2. b | 3. d | 4. d | 5. b |
| 6. d | 7. a | 8. c | 9. b | 10. d |

True/False

| 1. T | 2. F | 3. F | 4. F | 5. F |
| 6. T | 7. T | 8. T | 9. F | 10. T |

Completion

1.	denomination	6.	ethclass
2.	11%	7.	civil religion
3.	symbolic	8.	ethnicity; religion
4.	respectable bigotry	9.	social mobility
5.	Roman Catholicism	10.	Episcopalian

Chapter 6 – *The Native Americans*

Multiple Choice

1. d	2. b	3. a	4. d	5. c
6. d	7. a	8. c	9. d	10. b

True/False

1. T	2. T	3. F	4. T	5. F
6. F	7. F	8. T	9. F	10. F

Completion

1.	2; 22	6.	35 – 40
2.	Allotment Act	7.	23; 90
3.	setoffs	8.	crossover effect
4.	Pan-Indianism	9.	American Indian Religious Freedom
5.	internal colonialism	10.	millenarian movement

Chapter 7 – *The Making of African Americans in a White America*

Multiple Choice

1. d	2. a	3. c	4. b	5. d
6. b	7. c	8. d	9. b	10. d

True/False

1. T	2. T	3. F	4. T	5. F
6. F	7. F	8. F	9. T	10. T

Completion

1.	Ebonics	6.	CORE (The Congress of Racial Equality)
2.	Underground Railroad	7.	de jure
3.	Niagara Movement	8.	bus boycott
4.	talented tenth	9.	Black Power
5.	A. Philip Randolph	10.	Muslim

Chapter 8 – *African Americans Today*

Multiple Choice

1. b	2. c	3. c	4. a	5. b
6. d	7. d	8. a	9. b	10. c

True/False

1. F	2. T	3. T	4. F	5. F
6. F	7. T	8. F	9. F	10. T

Completion

1.	de facto		6.	Redlining
2.	25		7.	differential justice
3.	underemployed		8.	victimization surveys
4.	W.E.B. Du Bois		9.	gerrymandering
5.	class		10.	Fair Housing

Chapter 9 – *Hispanic Americans*

Multiple Choice

1. b	2. a	3. c	4. a	5. d
6. b	7. d	8. b	9. c	10. a

True/False

1. F	2. T	3. F	4. T	5. F
6. F	7. T	8. F	9. T	10. T

Completion

1.	panethnicity		6.	maquiladoras
2.	Cisnero v. Corpus Christi Independent School District		7.	freedom flotilla
3.	bilingual education		8.	Marielitos
4.	5		9.	color gradient
5.	migradollars		10.	brain drain

Chapter 10 – *Mexican Americans and Puerto Ricans*

Multiple Choice

1. b	2. d	3. d	4. a	5. c
6. c	7. c	8. c	9. a	10. b

True/False

1. F	2. T	3. T	4. T	5. F
6. T	7. T	8. T	9. T	10. F

Completion

1.	repatriation		6.	grape boycott
2.	La Raza		7.	agriculture
3.	20; 10		8.	third
4.	color gradient		9.	Reies Lope—z Tijerina
5.	culture of poverty		10.	pentecostalism

Chapter 11 – *Asian Americans: Growth and Diversity*

Multiple Choice

1. d	2. c	3. b	4. c	5. a
6. b	7. a	8. b	9. b	10. d

True/False

1. T	2. F	3. F	4. T	5. F
6. F	7. T	8. T	9. F	10. F

Completion

1.	ilchomose		6.	Haoles
2.	kye		7.	exogamy
3.	second		8.	Ka Lahui Hawaii
4.	Filipino		9.	middlemen
5.	gook syndrome		10.	Yellow Peril

Chapter 12 – *Chinese Americans and Japanese Americans*

Multiple Choice

1. b	2. d	3. b	4. d	5. a
6. c	7. c	8. d	9. a	10. b

True/False

1. F	2. F	3. F	4. T	5. T
6. F	7. T	8. F	9. F	10. T

Completion

1.	Alien Land Act	6.	tourism
2.	evacuees	7.	tongs
3.	Mitsuye Endo; United States	8.	Lilly Chen
4.	Civil Liberties Act	9.	Buddhist
5.	punks	10.	intermarriage

Chapter 13 – *Jewish Americans: Quest to Maintain Identity*

Multiple Choice

1. d	2. c	3. b	4. c	5. b
6. c	7. c	8. a	9. b	10. a

True/False

1. F	2. T	3. F	4. T	5. T
6. F	7. T	8. F	9. T	10. T

Completion

1.	anti-Semitism	6.	Zionism
2.	Judaization	7.	United Jewish Appeal
3.	fringes-of-values	8.	sacramental
4.	out-group vices	9.	kashrut
5.	Anti-Defamation League	10.	Yiddishkait

Chapter 14 – *Women: The Oppressed Majority*

Multiple Choice

1. b	2. d	3. a	4. d	5. b
6. c	7. a	8. c	9. c	10. d

True/False

1. T	2. T	3. F	4. F	5. F
6. F	7. T	8. F	9. T	10. F

Completion

1.	gender roles	6.	Displaced homemakers
2.	labeling approach	7.	thinking
3.	Nineteenth Amendment	8.	Roe; Wade
4.	feminine mystique	9.	double jeopardy
5.	glass ceiling	10.	nationalism

Chapter 15 – *Beyond the United States: The Comparative Perspective*

Multiple Choice

1. c	2. b	3. b	4. a	5. c
6. d	7. a	8. c	9. b	10. d

True/False

1. T	2. F	3. F	4. F	5. T
6. F	7. F	8. T	9. F	10. T

Completion

1. ethnonational
2. mestizo
3. color gradient
4. M—etis
5. home rule

6. Protestants
7. Diaspora
8. Law of Return
9. apartheid
10. Nelson Mandela

Chapter 16 – *Overcoming Exclusion*

Multiple Choice

1. c	2. b	3. b	4. a	5. c
6. d	7. a	8. b	9. c	10. d

True/False

1. T	2. T	3. F	4. T	5. F
6. F	7. F	8. F	9. F	10. T

Completion

1. White; female
2. 11
3. American Association of Retired Persons
4. 48
5. stigma

6. Americans with Disabilities
7. Alfred Kinsey
8. Homophobia
9. Bowers; Hardwick
10. gap